Feb. 27, 1987

Happy Birthday Mom.

May you relive the happy memories
his music has given thru this book.

Love,
Sharon & Ron

The Wonderful

Private World of

$\mathcal{L}$·I·B·E·R·A·C·E

The Wonderful Private World of

L·I·B·E·R·A·C·E

by Liberace

1817

HARPER & ROW, PUBLISHERS, New York

Cambridge, Philadelphia, San Francisco,

Washington, London, Mexico City,

São Paulo, Singapore, Sydney

HANNIBAL BOOKS, INC.

Copyright © 1986 by Liberace.

FIRST EDITION

Book design by Kathleen Westray and Ed Sturmer, Design and Printing Productions, New York.

Photo Research by Ilene Cherna Bellovin.

Library of Congress Cataloging-in-Publication Data
Liberace, 1919-   The wonderful private world of Liberace.
1. Liberace, 1919-   2. Pianists—United States—Biography.   I. Title.
ML417.L67A3   1986   786.1'092'4   [B]   85-42884
ISBN 0-06-015481-0

86 87 88 89 90   10 9 8 7 6 5 4 3 2 1

CONTENTS

*T*HIS book is going to be different from the other three I've written. For better or worse, it's the real thing. The other books were written in collaboration with somebody else. The trade term was "as told to." There was nothing wrong with that, but it was like playing the piano with four hands. Although a duet can be very pleasant, it's nowhere near as rewarding as a solo.

This latest effort deals with my private life, the offstage person very few people know about. It seems logical that I alone would be the one to reveal this other side of Liberace, the nonprofessional side, to tell it like it really is.

I've discovered that every performer—and I've known most of them in my time—is really two distinctly different people. I was first made aware of this several years ago, when I spent an unforgettable evening with the fabulous Mae West. It was at the time when my fifties television show was at the peak of its popularity. When asked what she wanted for her birthday, Miss West had replied, "Just bring me Liberace."

A mutual friend informed me, and we decided that I'd appear at her door on the night of her birthday with a huge red bow stretched across my chest. She lived in an apartment on Rossmore Avenue, in Hollywood. She owned the whole building. As you'll discover, an interest in real estate was something Miss West and I had in common.

"Surprise!" I cried. "I'm your birthday present."

Miss West laughed with pleasure and invited me into her living room. During that memorable evening, she told me the fascinating story of her life. I noticed she always spoke of herself in the third person, referring to Mae West as if she wasn't present. It didn't take me long to realize I actually wasn't with the world's greatest sex symbol. That Mae West was a self-creation who had captured the public's attention and become a legend never to be surpassed. She had made the word "sex" synonymous with "fun" and never "dirty." But the person with whom I was sharing these pleasurable hours was a sweet and dignified lady who did not drink, or smoke, or utter a single naughty word.

I find it equally natural to speak of "Mr. Showmanship" Liberace as if he were another person. The man behind the music, the glamour, the glitz, the man who has created a successful career spanning more than forty years, is another Liberace. He's the one you're going to meet in this book.

Above: A night on the town with the one and only Mae West.
Opposite: Behind my Malibu bar.

WHEN I started this book, I couldn't help wondering if I was doing it the right way. After all, it was so very different from the other books. One afternoon, I ran into Shirley MacLaine in a florist shop in Malibu. She'd never seen my Malibu place, so I invited her over. While we were having a drink, I discovered she had just completed her book *Dancing in the Light.* "What a coincidence," I said. "I'm just starting my fourth book."

She described a private place she had up in Washington, where she liked to sit outside, particularly when it was raining. She would sit under an umbrella and jot down the material in longhand. The solace and quietude of the place were very inspiring to writing in this personal style.

I told her I was doing mine in longhand, as well, just as if I was writing a letter to someone. She smiled encouragingly. "But that's exactly how you should do it!"

So here it is, a very personal letter from me to you, sharing an intimate glimpse into the wonderful private world of Liberace.

Liberace

Life on the Road

*F*OR most people, traveling means visiting new and exciting places, sightseeing, eating in fabulous restaurants. For a performer, traveling almost always means going on the road to play in places you've usually played before, room service, and the only sights being your hotels and the theaters. It also means countless interviews to promote the show. With very few exceptions, the press has been kind to me, and I have some good friends among them. But I do get tired of being asked the same things over and over again. I can't change the answers, because I like to be honest, so I wish they would change the questions. A typical interview usually goes like this:

Q. Do you really have a piano-shaped pool?

A. Not anymore. I sold it with the Sherman Oaks house in 1958.

Q. How do you react to criticism about wearing real fur coats?

A. I never wear furs of endangered species. All my furs were bred especially for the skins that go into making coats. Besides, they were dead when I bought them.

Q. I understand you were offered a major role in a movie that required nudity in several scenes. Is that true?

A. I'm more famous for putting on clothes than taking them off. Furthermore, when it comes to showing the body—let's face it—I'm no Arnold Swartzenegger.

Q. Have you had a face lift?

A. Not yet. But if you think I've already had one, it means I can still

What a way to go—in a coat
with a sixteen-foot train of
unendangered species.

afford to wait until my friend and authority on the subject, Phyllis Diller, tells me it's absolutely necessary.

Q. Is that your real hair?

A. The hair is real—but the color, only my hairdresser knows.

Q. How many pianos do you have?

A. It all depends on which house. But I do have one in my master bedroom. An upright grand. Just in case I wake up in the middle of the night and want to "tinkle."

Q. How do you stay so young?

A. When I think of people like George Burns and Bob Hope, who are still going strong in their eighties, I feel like a kid. And look at Cary Grant, who proves you can still be a sex symbol at eighty-two.

*T*HE late great vaudeville star Will Rogers once said, "I only know what I read in the papers." As you can see from the above, if you knew only what you read in the papers about me, you'd know very little. That was another reason I felt I had to write this book—to introduce me to you.

I'D always heard he travels fastest who travels alone. When I began to take my act on the road, I learned how wrong that was. At the very least, I have my conductor, stage manager, valet-dresser, two propmen. When I bring along guest artists, the troupe can get to be as large as fourteen or sixteen. And when they bring along wives, husbands, parents, or whatevers—well, you can just imagine!

You might think that when a group like this is together in a strange city, it's like a big family. The truth is, when you work and travel with people every single day, you want to get away from them. Each person has his or her own outlet. One might like to go to museums, another to the movies, another to the gym or shopping, and some might just want to be alone and do nothing.

It's not easy to bring all these different types of people together in a compatible way. Once or twice during each tour, I'll give a dinner party, because it sounds festive. When I invite each one, they ask who's coming, and when I reply—the gang—they respond, "Eehhh! that's not such a big deal." I try to make up for the lack of enthusiasm

by taking them to an exciting restaurant, a place that's unusual or glamorous. Believe me, in some towns that can be pretty hard to find.

So, you see, after the glitter and excitement of the performance, and the warmth of the audience, there's usually nothing to do but go back to the hotel. From what is printed in the papers and from my costumes and shows, most people think I'm a bird of exotic plumage. The truth is I'm a nester, and I hate living in hotels, I get very home-sick. No matter how gorgeous they are, they're still hotels. If I could, I'd probably buy a house or apartment in every city in which I play. As that's impossible, I try to create a homelike atmosphere in my suite. I put my own towels out and sometimes even use my own bed linens. I take anything that looks like advertising material and put it in an empty drawer. I put out photographs of my family, friends, and dogs. I have my own ashtrays and knickknacks around. These little touches help to turn the impersonal though often beautiful suite of "Mr. Showmanship" into the more private world of Liberace.

Ever since I first went on the road in the early forties, I've felt this urge to turn hotels into temporary homes. I remember a sixteen-week engagement at Chicago's Palmer House in 1947. A suite was included in my contract, and I immediately went into my act of get-ting rid of everything that had a hotel logo on it and replacing it with my own things, right down to the stationery.

The suite had two bathrooms, and I coaxed the housekeeping staff into transforming one of them into a makeshift kitchen. Since I carried my own utensils—pots, pans, and dishes—all they had to supply was a refrigerator and an electric stove, which were placed on a temporary platform over the bathtub. My work table was over the john, which was completely hidden by a long, white tablecloth.

The Palmer House press agent was crazy about my "kitchen" and arranged a photo layout for the *Chicago Tribune* of me cooking in it. When the photographer asked me to step back to enable him to get a better angle, I accidentally flushed the toilet in the process. We all got a big laugh out of it and, fortunately, the sound effect didn't show in the picture.

Actually, I turned out some very good dinners in that kitchen. You can be sure I was careful to avoid the flusher whenever I invited my co-workers, the Merial Abbott Dancers, and an attractive young couple making their debuts in my show in the Empire Room, Marge and Gower Champion. Also sharing the bill was a young singer who became the father of twins during the engagement. Later in his career, he became the famous talk-show host Mike Douglas.

Below: Working in my improvised kitchen on the road.

Above: The very friendly English birds
in Trafalgar Square.

At the end of the run, I returned the suite to its original condition. I packed all my kitchen and cooking supplies in their fitted Halliburton luggage cases, and no one was the wiser.

I remember doing my settling-in thing at the Père Marquette Hotel, in Peoria, Illinois, where I was engaged to appear for the whole of the spring and summer of 1948. Something happened that made that stay a particularly memorable one. Around the Easter holiday, some friends presented me with six adorable baby ducklings. They knew how much I love pets, which bring out all of my paternal instincts and become my "children." These darling little balls of yellow fluff were no exceptions. From the beginning, they had individual personalities. I gave the more playful ones the Disneylike names Donald, Daffy, and Daisy. The more sedate ones got the glamorous names Dietrich, Garbo, and Rita (as in Hayworth).

Ever the decorator, I created a duck "mansion" for them out of cardboard boxes and wallpaper samples. Over the weeks, as I watched them grow into full-fledged white ducks, I fell more and more in love with them. They made the most wonderful, affectionate pets. I always had little treats for them, which they would eat out of the palm of my hand. When I called out their names, they would come to me. When I returned to my rooms after the show, I could see six pairs of webbed feet sticking out through the crack at the bottom of the door, and what a quacking-good greeting I'd get upon entering.

The maid also became very attached to them during her daily visits to make up the rooms. She lived on a farm outside the city and, when my engagement was over, I left my six feathery friends with her. Before handing them over, I made her promise she would never eat them but keep them as pets for as long as they lived. Believe me, I shed a tear when I had to bid them farewell and put them out for adoption.

T HE hotel staff and I always get very friendly, especially during the longer engagements. Maybe it's because they think it's kind of marvelous that I always try to make a home for myself whenever I have to live in a place for any length of time. Maybe it's because they appreciate the fact that I'm the type who straightens up the rooms before the maids arrive. I've even had maids who've taken my laundry home, washed it, and brought it back the next day, all perfectly ironed and folded. I guess the extra service is why a member of the troupe once teasingly called me "the chambermaid's delight."

There was one unforgettable occasion when the friendliness of a maid got just a little out of control. It was during one of my engagements in Louisville, Kentucky. I had a very nice suite of rooms in a charming hotel in the downtown area. The management had even brought in a brand-new grand piano for the living room, on which I could practice in private.

One day, my musical director at that time, Gordon Robinson, asked if he could use the piano to rehearse a new aria with my singing star, Jean Fenn, of the Metropolitan Opera. Bright and early the next morning, they arrived at the suite. I showed them into the living room, ordered some coffee, and told them to make themselves at home. They began rehearsing the lovely "Un bel dì" from Puccini's *Madama Butterfly*.

After excusing myself, I went into the bathroom off the master bedroom, hung my robe on the door, and proceeded with my morning ritual. I was sitting on the john, totally nude, when the maid entered the bathroom. Surprised and embarrassed, I asked her to leave.

Below: The billboard for the engagement in which Jean Fenn sang her unforgettable "Un Bel Di." Only Jean and I got the joke.

I may have been unnerved, but she obviously wasn't. Without making any move to go, she said, "I thought you were playing the piano."

"As you can see, I'm not."

"Well, then, who is playing?"

"My musical director," I said. By this time, I was trying to hide myself by contorting my body into a fetal position. She was completely oblivious to the situation and went on like a contestant in a game of "Twenty Questions," while I stupidly sat there and answered her.

She asked, "Who is that singing?"

"That's Jean Fenn."

She shook her head. "Don't believe I ever heard of her."

"She's with the Metropolitan Opera."

"What's that song she's singing?"

" 'Un bel dì.' "

She frowned. "What's that mean?"

" 'One Fine Day,' " I cried, still not believing what was happening. If there had been a chair handy, I'm sure she'd have pulled it over and sat down.

"Is she gonna sing that song in your show?"

"She's planning to."

"Will you be playing for her?"

I nodded. She leaned over conspiratorially. "I don't suppose you could arrange a couple of complimentary tickets for me?"

Shrinking back, I replied, "If you'll leave your name with me, I'll see what I can do."

"I'll give it to you right now. Do you have a piece of paper I can write it on?"

"Not handy," I said, adding forcefully, "perhaps you can leave it for me later. Now, if you'll excuse me, I'd like to take a shower."

She finally got the point. "Okay." As she reached the door, she turned and asked, "Will I see you later?"

I nodded. "Yes. *Later.*"

Before I could get up and lock the door, she was back in the room. "I brought you some extra towels."

"Thank you," I said, grabbing one and trying to cover myself.

After she'd left, I was finally able to take my shower. After dressing, I hurried into the living room, calling, "Gordon! Jean! You won't believe this."

I told them the whole story. Jean said, "I'll never be able to sing 'Un bel dì' again without thinking about what happened to you in your bathroom."

They both began to laugh hysterically. That was the end of rehearsal for that day.

Opposite: The master bathroom in my Las Vegas home.

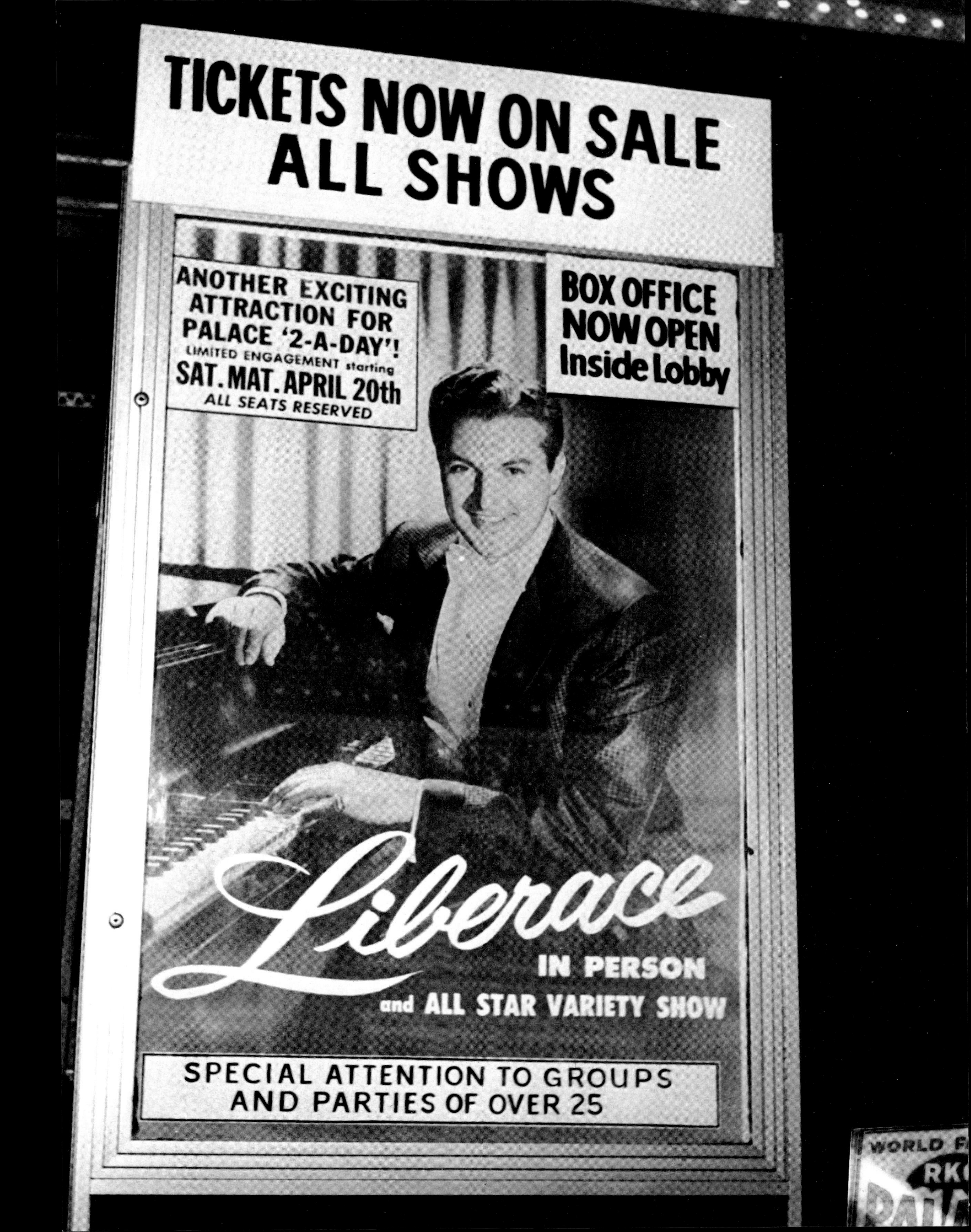
TICKETS NOW ON SALE
ALL SHOWS
ANOTHER EXCITING
ATTRACTION FOR
PALACE '2-A-DAY'!
LIMITED ENGAGEMENT starting
SAT. MAT. APRIL 20th
ALL SEATS RESERVED
BOX OFFICE
NOW OPEN
Inside Lobby
Liberace
IN PERSON
and ALL STAR VARIETY SHOW
SPECIAL ATTENTION TO GROUPS
AND PARTIES OF OVER 25
WORLD FA
RKO

The Showplace of the Nation

*I*N the golden days of vaudeville, the dream of every performer was to headline at the Palace Theatre in New York. Nowadays, everybody wants to play Radio City Music Hall in New York, the theater that's known as "the showplace of the nation." My first engagement there was the culmination of four years of discussions that started in 1980, when the Rockettes were featured in one of my Las Vegas shows.

My stage managers and agents were all against Radio City. They had a dozen good arguments why I shouldn't do it.

—Play Long Island. That's like New York. And you won't be taking any chances.

—Do you realize there are six thousand seats in that place? What if you do only half a house? It'll hurt you career-wise.

—Stay in the hinterlands. Stay out of the big cities.

—You know the New York press. If they don't like you, they'll murder you.

Those were the chances I was going to have to take. They were either going to love me or hate me, but that was the story of my life. You can't stand still. No matter how successful you are, it's fleeting unless you do something to sustain it. My good friend Barbra Streisand once put it just right. "You never stop auditioning."

I felt sure I could do it. When you give out positive waves, have an aura of confidence about something you want to do, you're fortified by all the experience in the past. It reminded me of what had happened after the first time I played Carnegie Hall in New York. Every-

Announcing my Palace Theatre engagement thirty years before and just four blocks away from the record-breaking Radio City Music Hall engagement.

Above: A date with Judy—the one and
only Judy Garland.

body was predicting I could play there for a week if I wanted to. I said, "I don't want to. I want to play Madison Square Garden."

They told me I was crazy. The Garden was for prizefights and circuses. But I'd done my homework at the public library, and I was ready for them. I said, "Paderewski played in Madison Square Garden. If it was good enough for him, it's good enough for me."

I did follow the circus into Madison Square Garden. I mean—I literally followed the elephants. They were taking them down the ramp when I came in for rehearsals on the afternoon of my concert. All I could say was, "I hope it doesn't smell like this tonight."

It didn't, but that didn't stop the audience from coming tongue in cheek. Were they kidding, trying to fill Madison Square Garden with a piano player? We did. It was a sellout, and it was history making. Since then, lots of acts have played both the old and new Garden: Judy Garland, the Rolling Stones, Michael Jackson, even Pavarotti.

The first Radio City date in 1984 was over thirty years after the Garden and almost thirty years after my last New York City appearance. The engagement set a box-office and attendance record for the first six months of 1984. Nobody had ever played for twenty-one consecutive performances before, and certainly nobody had ever sold them out before.

They asked me to do the show again the following year. They picked out the same season and intended to use the same group sales force. I can recall sitting at a Board of Directors meeting, listening to speeches about letting lightning strike twice. They wanted me to do the same show, believed that the same people would come back to see it again. I agreed that, if they would, it would be wonderful. Repeat business is great. Finally, I asked if they'd like to know what I really wanted to do. There were certain things I would repeat, because I thought the audience would expect to see them. But I also wanted to dance with the Rockettes, which I hadn't done, do a number with six pianos, and, most of all, make more of the Easter holiday. For my appearance, they cut the annual Easter show for the first time in twenty-seven years. At first, they had wanted the Easter Pageant and me. That would have made a show that ran four hours, which is too long to expect an audience to sit through. I said, "You can have either the Resurrection, or you can have Liberace. But you can't have both."

HE date for my return engagement was set. April 4, 1985. The day before, something happened that had the whole town talking. There was a front-page story in the *New York*

Times, headlined "Liberace Is Here, With His Glitter Undimmed." It was absolutely precedent shattering. About the only way an entertainer makes the front page of the *Times* is with a little box in the corner that announces you can read about him on the obituary page.

The day after the opening, both the New York *Daily News* and the *Post* ran pictures on their front pages. All the reviews were fabulous. Not only did the engagement break my own Radio City record, it also set a fifty-three-year record for the theater.

Below: Struttin' my stuff with the Rockettes.

A lot of things came together in my mind during and just after that second Music Hall engagement that made me decide to make some changes. The rewards from my career have been phenomenal, a life style that includes every luxury: several magnificent homes, custom cars, exquisite jewelry, an elegant personal wardrobe in addition to the glamorous show costumes, and many fine pianos, as well as a shopping center, a museum, and a restaurant. But when did I get to enjoy all these things? I was always working. I finally said to myself, "Liberace, it's time to smell the roses. If you don't slow down, you just might wind up being the richest piano player in the cemetery."

I'd been playing everything from night clubs, to concert halls, to theaters, to sports arenas. My bookers kept sneaking me into these barns, where I followed the Harlem Globetrotters. I had to keep modifying my act, eliminating things that couldn't work in certain situations.

Now, I've no intention of retiring, but I have decided to retire those engagements where I can't do my very best, which was what I'd just done in New York. There aren't many places like the Music Hall— maybe ten in the entire North American continent—and the others may not be as glamorous, but they do offer the facilities to do a great production. Although it takes courage to turn down lucrative contracts that would enable me to increase my income—and also pay more taxes—my acceptance of any engagement would be based on its being an event that would enhance my career and give maximum pleasure to my audience, rather than just being another job. By not being too available, I'd also prevent overexposure and ensure longevity in both popularity and health.

The health issue really did play a part in my decision. When I got back to Las Vegas, I made an appointment with my personal physi-

Opposite: A quiet evening at home. Below: Outside Radio City Music Hall with the announcement of my Easter engagement.

cian, Dr. Elias Ghanem, for a long-overdue complete physical examination. He was concerned over reports that I'd lost thirty pounds rather rapidly on a—would you believe—"watermelon diet." In subsequent testing, he discovered I'd robbed my system of essential nutrients, which was causing me to experience a let down in my normally high energy level. He immediately placed me on a nutritional program augmented by super-vitamin supplements. Later tests showed such a dramatic improvement that Dr. Ghanem said, "Not only do you have the stamina of a thirty-year-old athlete, but you'll live to be a hundred."

Some of this testing required special equipment and had to be performed in a local hospital. As a result, false rumors started to circulate about my health. According to the gossips, you name it, and I had it.

Let me assure you, I've never felt better in my life!

I'D noticed that recently audiences were getting more and more of a kick out of the little stories I'd tell during the show about incidents that had happened in my private life. It was then that I decided to accept an offer to write a book about all of the wonderful things I've never before told about my life offstage. Unlike Shirley MacLaine, who needed to find a private place to write in, I already had private places, including a hideaway in Las Vegas. The thing I needed most was the time to do it. Monetary success brings tremendous obligations to others, to the people who help to guide my career, to the many individuals and their families who depend on me for a livelihood. Somewhere along the line, I decided I had an obligation to myself, to start enjoying the things I've worked so hard to acquire during the many exciting and exhausting show-business years. And, of course, there was this book to be written, the one you're reading at this very minute.

I announced to all of the people involved in my career that I was doing the book but didn't want it to be something for which I grabbed

Below: Even diamonds need a bath!

a few moments here and there. I wanted to take six months off for the book. It shocked the hell out of everybody. Aside from anything else, nobody had ever heard of Liberace taking six weeks off, let alone six months. Sometimes, I even have trouble remembering six consecutive days in which there have been no business conferences, no costume fittings, no interviews, no rehearsals, no performances.

The business people wanted to know how I expected to pay my salaries, make my mortgage payments, meet all the financial obligations incurred by my many homes and business interests. I asked how much money I'd made during the previous year. When they told me, even I was surprised. I said, "I think that's enough to take care of things."

If I ran short, there were institutions that would advance the money, based on my collateral and my reputation as an entertainer. If I had to borrow, I would borrow. I was not going to worry about those things. I couldn't plan my future according to figures in a ledger. It was pointed out to me that even if this book became the biggest best-seller in the world, it could never earn the money that I was giving up by not working for six months. All I had to do was agree to the offers that were already on my desk, to earn over two million dollars. Some of the press picked up on the story. That only added fuel to the rumors. Something had to be wrong with Liberace for him to turn down that much money.

It's funny how things happen sometimes. I was doing this book because it would enhance my sense of self, do something for me as a person and not merely my career. You can't always do that with mere dollars and cents. But money does have a momentum of its own. To my astonishment, I found I could sit down and smell the roses and write my book, and still make money, which is like having the best of all possible worlds.

During my six-month "holiday," somebody approached me about getting into licensing. I didn't know what he was talking about. He explained that it was product endorsement, the sort of thing Gloria Vanderbilt and Bill Blass and people like that make a fortune doing. He thought I was a natural for things like clothes and jewelry lines, to say nothing of fragrances. As it happened, a Frenchman had already created formulas for a men's cologne and ladies' perfume especially for me. This Liberace scent was blended of secret elements signifying the glitz and glamour, as well as the homespun quality signified by my love of cooking and decorating. It's so secret that they've locked it away in a Swiss vault. They're going to start production in the very near future.

I've taken time to smell the roses and, in the words of the great Styne-Sondheim song, "Everything's Coming Up Roses."

Below: With Tony Bennett.

Opposite: Time to smell the roses.

I Lost My Virginity at Sixteen

J PROMISED I'd tell some stories that have never been told before. Well, this certainly is one of them. This year marks the golden anniversary of the loss of my virginity, and it's worth a little celebrating. If it hadn't been for the Depression, I probably would not have started my career as early as I did, and if I hadn't started my career while still a teenager, I surely would never have met Miss Bea Haven (say it fast). But that's getting a little ahead of the story.

During the twenties, my father had been a very successful concert French-horn player, playing in the large symphonic orchestras that underscored silent films in the great movie palaces of the day and touring with other great orchestras. The stock market crash and talkies collectively put an end to his career. The "luxury" of serious music was one of the first things eliminated by the public. They didn't feel it was a necessary commodity, and attendance fell off. Dad was a musical purist and wouldn't play with dance bands, so there he was, sitting home without a job. We were a family of four children, and the burden of supporting it fell on the rest of us, except for my younger brother, Rudy, who was just out of kindergarten. My mother had given him Rudolph Valentino's first name, just as she'd given the star's last name to me as a middle name. Mom was some fan! She was also very resourceful about finding ways to earn money. First, she ran a grocery store and then, a fruit and vegetable market. She worked in

A young me dreaming of the future, but never dreaming how wonderful it would be.

a cookie factory, too. I can remember her sitting at the kitchen table with a very strong light, doing clock embroidery on ladies' hosiery. It was very painstaking work, but nothing was too difficult if it would help keep us in food, shelter, and clothes.

The older children also did their share. My older brother, George, played the violin in dance bands. My sister, Angie, took whatever jobs came her way. Although I was barely in my teens during this difficult period, I couldn't wait to start working and contributing my share. I tried to make myself look older by wearing some of George's "big band" uniforms. I thought they made me look worldly and sophisticated. Obviously, I didn't fool anybody, because I had a so-called baby face. In some of my early publicity photographs, it looked as if the mother's milk was still on my lips. I started by taking weekend jobs, playing the piano with three or four other musicians. Dad was very particular about where I played and how I earned my money, not only because I was so young but because of his dreams of a serious concert

Below: Mom behind the counter at her (Nina's) Fruit Shoppe which she expanded into a grocery and deli through her hard work.
Opposite: A rose for a queen, with Mom in Las Vegas.

career for me. He would drive me out beforehand to have a look at the place that wanted to hire us. It'd often look like any other innocent ice cream parlor, and he'd give his approval. What he didn't know was that there was a speakeasy back room, where all the dancing and drinking went on, for this was still during Prohibition. I can still recall the first time I ever saw a lady smoke. It was in one of those "ice cream parlors." I was so shocked that I stopped playing. I'd never seen anything like it before in my whole life.

Soon, everybody except Dad was out there making a buck. At the end of the week, we'd all sit in the kitchen, put our salaries on the table, and budget our incomes to keep the family going. My poor father resented this, because he felt he wasn't carrying his share of the load. He began to do lots of crazy little things, like hiding the alarm clock so my mother would be late for work and maybe lose her job. He didn't mean anything evil. It was just that he was such a proud man.

Dad had a friend who was an agent and who'd call and ask him if he could get his son to play a private party or club date. That could mean I'd make about twenty-five dollars, just for playing one night.

Below: With Suzanne France, my singing coach.
Opposite: George and me with our proud Papa.

3 8

During the thirties, people felt lucky if they could make twenty-five dollars for working a whole week. As time went on, some of my "gigs" got pretty racy for a teenager. I'll never forget the first time I got on a bus with a bunch of girl "dancers." I'd been engaged to accompany them, and I asked for their music. They all had the same routine: waltzes and slow numbers for the first time they came out, fox-trots for the second time, and something fast as lightning for their third appearance. This was the classic accompaniment for strippers, which was what they were. I tell you—it was an education!

Below: The Liberaces—me, Mom and George.

I often got jobs in the same clubs where my brother George was playing in the band. This made my parents feel much easier about my work, because George would be there to act as chaperone for the "baby." One memorable time, we were appearing at Sam Pick's Club Madrid on the outskirts of Milwaukee. This was one of our classier jobs. The big night clubs of the day all had an orchestra plus a floor show featuring a soubrette or pop singer, a prima donna who did the light opera numbers, and a blues singer who sang songs like "Body and Soul" and "Love for Sale." My job was to accompany the singers as they went around the room between shows, singing requests from the audience. People would tip them five or ten dollars for each number, and they would split whatever they got with me.

Above: George and me in the days when costumes were much cheaper.

At the Club Madrid, George's first wife was the soubrette. She was very cute and talented and very friendly with the blues singer, Miss Bea Haven, who was a very sexy lady. George had to play until closing, but the singers and I were finished after the second show. I didn't drive yet, and Miss Bea Haven very kindly offered to drive me home in her car, because George wouldn't be through until after two in the morning.

Invariably, the conversations during those drives would turn to sex. One night, she couldn't help noticing I was visibly aroused. She pulled over to the side of the road and took "advantage" of me. I must admit I loved every minute of it, and it became a frequent happening. The lady especially enjoyed my "encores," and those drives got longer and longer. She was twice my age and very experienced but she made me feel grown up and manly at last. After that, being around girls my own age didn't excite me at all. Compared to Miss Bea Haven, they all seemed so adolescent.

The thrill of making it with an older woman diminished as I grew older. Younger girls started to represent more of a challenge, probably because of their comparative innocence.

I only hope I can do as well as George Burns when I reach his age. Have you ever seen him with an older woman? He claims that's because there aren't many women his age who are still around. He says it now takes him all night to do what he used to do all night long. More power to him! He's ninety and an inspiration to young guys like me who are still in their sixties.

Below: At a family picnic in my late teens.
Opposite: George and me.
Overleaf Left: A studio portrait of the Liberace kids, George, Angie and me.
Overleaf Right: George and Angie less than happy on their mount.

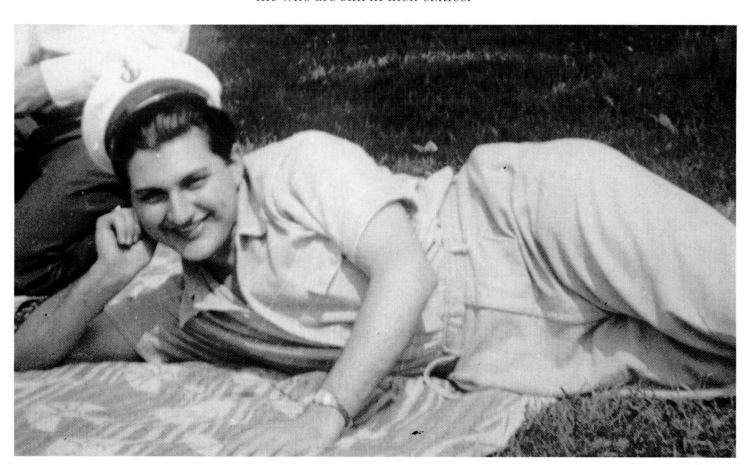

Above: That's me at the piano with the high school mixer orchestra.

*T*HINKING back on that difficult period, I find there was a lot in it that was good, especially the way we Liberace kids loved and looked after each other—George, and me, and later my kid brother, Rudy, and of course my one and only sister, Angie. When we were very young, there was a lot of competition between Angie and me, and it all centered on the good, old upright piano in the living room. How we used to fight over who was going to practice! She had a few years' head start on me and was determined not to let me catch up. I sat by, waiting for my turn, while she played the same piece over and over just to antagonize me. Our mother often had to come in to be the timekeeper and referee. In spite of her attitude toward practicing, Angie didn't have the dedication necessary to become a professional musician, while I seemed to have been born with it. She finally quit taking lessons and, as time went by, became very supportive of my musical ambitions.

Angie got married and started having her babies, Diane and Fred, just as I was beginning to play my first professional club dates. At about the same time that Miss Bea Haven was teaching me one set of facts of life, I was learning another by being built-in baby sitter for Angie's children. I was changing their diapers and, as they got older, dressing them and even making Diane's curls. I loved those kids as if they were my own, and Angie felt very safe leaving them in my care. One of the great joys of my later success was that it enabled me to help put Fred through medical school. To this day, Angie's children and grandchildren are among the closest members of my family.

During the fifties, when the children were old enough to be on their own, Angie gave up a fine career as an X-ray technician to accompany me on my tours. She was my secretary, my wardrobe mistress, and my all-'round Girl Friday. In her eyes, I was an idol as well as a brother.

I was playing an engagement at the Fontainebleau Hotel, in Miami Beach, during its heyday. Angie and I were staying in an eight-hundred-dollar-a-day suite (which was in my contract) and living in grand style. Unbeknownst to me, she had received a letter from my business manager asking her to try to get me to cut down on expenses. Angie knew very well I was of an extravagant nature. She decided to pitch in and help out by doing my personal laundry instead of sending it out and paying the exorbitant prices the hotel charged for washing shirts, shorts, socks, and the like.

Below: Mom making sure her boy looks his best for his Madison Square Garden engagement.

Above: Caught by the neighborhood
photographer with my favorite teddy
bear.
Opposite: With Angie after Radio City
opening.

On one of Angie's laundry days, I went out to lunch with friends and then did some shopping. All of the merchandise was sent to the hotel and, after I had returned, the bell captain asked if he could deliver the packages to my suite. Angie quickly took down her makeshift clothesline to avoid embarrassing me. When she answered the door, there were five bellboys carrying my purchases. She quietly did the necessary tipping and, once they were gone, made me aware of the letter about my expenses. She could not comply with the request to be more frugal about spending, unless I cooperated. That was the last time she ever did my laundry in the bathtub.

THERE was another incident that happened at the Fontainebleau, involving a very different kind of dirty laundry. I was very upset about a magazine article that had made fun of me in a derogatory way. The famous and powerful columnist Walter Winchell was in the audience on the night I tried to defend myself on the stage. It was so painful that I did it without a trace of humor. When I saw Walter after the show, he said, "Kid, don't ever fight your battles in front of an audience. Nobody wants it. There's only one place for dirty laundry, and that's the Laundromat. If you can make it entertaining, that's fine. But don't do it deadpan seriously."

It was one of the great lessons of my life. I thought of the times when I'd seen performers start getting on a soap box onstage; I was so embarrassed for them, I felt like getting under the table. So what if the public has read something a little nasty about me? It's in the back of their minds. They may have totally forgotten it. Why bring it up? They've come to be entertained and have fun, and my job—my only job—is to see that they get what they came for.

ANGIE stayed on the road with me for at least a year, and those were the days when I worked about forty weeks out of each year. We both felt the work was really too much for one woman. She still kids me about it. She says, "After I left, it took four people to replace me."

She's very nearly right about that.

CHAPTER 4

Vacations in Reverse

*M*OST people leave home to go on vacation. I do just the opposite. I've spent so much of my life on the road, performing in most of the world's greatest cities and resorts. But that's work. For a holiday, there's no place like home, especially since I have homes in some very interesting and exciting places. As I write this book, I have homes in six areas; by the time you read it—who knows? When I fall in love with a locale, I want to be able to put down roots and live there. It may seem like wild extravagance, but the truth is, I've never lost money in real estate yet. Even if I had, when I think of the special holidays each of these homes has afforded me, it would be worth it.

Depending on the season, the weather, or even my mood, I can have vacations at home that are comparable to a season in Monte Carlo (my Las Vegas place), a Caribbean cruise (in Malibu), a Hawaiian holiday (Palm Springs), Saint Moritz in Switzerland (Lake Tahoe), plus the dazzle and pace of the penthouses in Los Angeles and the Trump Tower in the heart of New York City. Imagine having the privilege of selecting one of these places in which to enjoy relaxation in privacy, without the exposure that surrounds a person in the public eye.

I'm fortunate enough to have so many interests that my holidays at home fly by. I can't find the time to do many of the things I really enjoy. Painting used to give me lots of pleasure. I loved to paint on

In the garden of my
Hollywood mansion.

fabrics and give things like ties and blouses to friends as gifts. It was a wonderful hobby for me. People seemed to enjoy receiving something handmade from me. The requests for my work became so large I either had to spend every spare minute filling them or give it up altogether. I also used to love to make all my own Christmas cards, but the list got so long that it became impossible.

O N vacation, most celebrities prefer to hide away from the public. This can lead to a very frustrating way of life. For myself, I enjoy being recognized and giving people autographs, with two exceptions. If I'm having dinner, I ask them to return after I've finished eating. I also refuse to sign when I'm in the men's room. After all, there's a time and place for everything.

I'd hate to be a recluse when I'm vacationing at home. Actually, I'm quite visible, doing my own shopping and marketing, attending local charitable and social events, going to movies, theaters, and clubs, or entertaining those friends I'm out of touch with when I'm working. I love to prepare a gourmet dinner and entertain at home, but I also enjoy inviting friends to my very own Tivoli Gardens Restaurant in Las Vegas and playing the host. Of course, I'm very much on display at the restaurant. It seems as if everyone brings a camera with them just in case I might be present, which is often the case, since I both "vacation" and work in Las Vegas. I enjoy posing for and with them, because I love meeting people on a personal level.

Sometimes, this leads to very amusing encounters with customers. One very sweet, elderly lady had just finished lunch at a table near mine. She was with a group of friends, all of whom were in their golden years. On their way out, they stopped to say hello. This very senior charmer paid me an unusual compliment. "Mr. Liberace, I want you to know you were one of my mother's favorites."

Opposite: An intimate corner in my Hollywood penthouse.
Overleaf: Movies at home in the days before the VCR.

I F you want to find me when I'm on vacation, try the local garage sales and flea markets. I love to go to them. No matter how much money they have, everybody loves a bargain and will go out searching for it. That includes Jackie Onassis and Liberace. I used to be a compulsive shopper. If I saw something in a

Above: Visiting Rosemary Clooney on the set of "White Christmas." Rosie has her fingers crossed hoping for the big hit it turned out to be.

Opposite: The artist at work on the mural in his home.

shop, I had to have it then and there, and I didn't care how much it cost. I've learned (well, more or less) that if you look around long enough, you'll find the same article at a fraction of the original cost. And it's lots of fun. I look for Rodeo Drive merchandise in discount stores. Believe it or not, I find it: the same labels, the same everything.

Finding a bargain is fascinating. In Palm Springs, I have some icons I brought back from Greece. I'd paid less than a hundred dollars for them. When I got home, I had them cleaned and appraised for insurance purposes. Those icons are worth thousands of dollars. I felt very proud that I'd found them in a dusty little shop in a little hideaway street in Athens. It turned out to be the same shop in which Jackie Onassis had bought her icons. I'll bet she felt as pleased with her "find" as I was with mine.

Making something out of nothing can also be a lot of fun. I found a little lamp at a garage sale for three dollars. It needed a shade, so when I got it home, I took a little vegetable basket, turned it upside down, and trimmed it with flowers. It turned out so attractive that people are always oohing and aahing and asking where I got it. In my Palm Springs home, you'll find the three-dollar lamp as well as a forty-two-thousand-dollar collection of glassware. There's a little bit of this and a little bit of that and, somehow, it all fits together, it blends. I guess it's because I love it all—the rare and valuable as well as the thrift shop "treasures."

———

*A*S you can guess from the number of homes I've done in my time, decorating is one of my greatest passions. They say everybody's a would-be decorator, but when I attempt something, I really study it. I'm self-taught in most things, except music.

I don't know where it came from, but I have this knack for being able to walk into raw space and getting a vision of what it will be like when it's done over. All it takes is four walls and some imagination. It doesn't have to be a thing of beauty when you find it to make a thing of beauty out of it. As a matter of fact, the worse it is, the more of a challenge it is to me. It's been like that with most of the places I've owned. The old mansion I used to have in Hollywood had been abandoned for ten years. Everybody wanted to know what I wanted with that place. The only thing they could think of was to tear it down. But the moment I walked in I could see the whole place as it would be when I was finished with it. By the time I was ready for a housewarming,

Left: My bedroom in Las Vegas with the
Sistine Chapel ceiling.

that's exactly what it looked like. The same thing in Palm Springs. They were going to tear it down to create a parking lot for the neighboring Catholic church and Jewish temple. That was before I came along and revitalized it to the point where it's the pride of the neighborhood.

A lot of people will say you can make anything beautiful if you have enough money. To that I can only reply that I've been in some "great mansions" where my only reaction was you can make anything ugly if you have enough money. The people who've owned these houses had no vision of their own and just turned it all over to the most expensive and "in" decorator around. Beauty really is in the eye of the beholder. All you need is to hang on to your vision and to find the right craftsmen and contractors to make it real. If you take time to look for them, these workmen are out there and not necessarily the most expensive in the yellow pages.

It's not just the money. I've worked with very nondescript and inexpensive places, like my hideaway in Las Vegas. People come in and say—oh, what a dream house, what a dollhouse! It's like heaven to walk in here. And it's really just one of several ordinary condominiums. When the owners saw what I'd done, they asked me to do some models for them. I replied I'd love to, but I was too busy at the time. All I wanted was to prove to myself what could be done to turn very simple surroundings into a thing of beauty without spending a fortune.

Opposite: The one-of-a-kind table made by Baccarat in Paris, in 1850, for an Indian Maharaja.
Below: Some of my treasures displayed on a Boule commode.
Overleaf: The pool area of my house high above Sunset Boulevard.

6 2

The challenge always gets to me. When I first walked into the penthouse in Los Angeles a few years ago, it hadn't been lived in for over seventeen years. It was what you'd call a dump. Most people would have said you had to be crazy to want to live in the place. The pool was filled with algae and debris. It was something out of the movie *Sunset Boulevard*. I just said, "This is it. I'll take it. I can make something beautiful out of it." I think the photographs prove I succeeded.

In case anybody is thinking Liberace will buy anything as long as it has some walls and a roof, let me say there are some places I'll walk away from no matter what visions of grandeur they conjure up in my mind. My rule of thumb is I won't buy a place that's condemned or unsafe in any way. I stay away from anything that's on stilts or in an endangered area. I couldn't handle natural disasters, like houses sliding down mountainsides or washing into the sea.

Below: The living room at the Hollywood penthouse.
Opposite: We literally had to raise the roof to get that chandelier in place.

With that attitude you might ask me what I'm doing in Malibu, where mud slides, ravine fires, floods, and earthquakes seem to be a way of life. The simple answer is I love Malibu. I've had three experiences there. The first place I bought was a simple condominium. I made it as beautiful as I could and would have been very happy, except for all my friends warning me about the mud slides that were happening to the right, left, and behind me. They finally scared me enough to sell my home back to the man who had built the building. I was happy with my two-hundred-percent profit, and he was equally happy with the showplace he got for his money.

After a while, I began to miss Malibu and thought it would be sensible if I had an income property out there. There was a complex with an owner's apartment and seventeen rental units that filled the bill.

While we were in negotiations, the rains came. A mud slide forty feet under the ground was pushing the property one inch closer to the sea every twenty-four hours. We were about to close on the building when it was condemned, and all of the tenants had to move out. That was one time I didn't follow my own rule and came within a hair of being stuck with a costly mistake.

Eventually, I found a place within a mile of my first Malibu apartment. This time, I was not going to take any chances and had some friends who were very knowledgeable about the area check it out. The report was that it was both sturdily built and not in danger of having some muddy hill smash it into the sea.

It was a six-unit condominium, and I bought the lower half. What I love most about it is that the water actually comes right under the deck. It's just like being on a boat. The ever-changing patterns of water and sky are fascinating. Even when it's foggy, it has a charm.

The helicopters and planes have to pass that way to get to the airport, and it's lovely to see all those little lights at night twinkling amid the stars. I adore it, even if some of my friends ask if I ever get seasick.

Even before the purchase was completed, I knew what I wanted to do in the way of decorating. I threw two of the units together to make a huge apartment and have the third as a guest house. The guest quarters have a totally different feeling from my own condo, softer and more feminine, because it's often rented by a lady; so, you see, I do have an income property after all.

I LOVE the gift of being able to see a room or house and erase the ugliness and just see the potential beauty. My former musical director and his wife had a lovely small home in Burbank. When they invited me over, the first thing that struck me was that there was too much furniture for the space. Jean, the wife, knew it and said, "Lee, I have too much furniture in here. What do you think?"

I replied, "If you really want to know, that entire wall has to be pushed out about ten feet."

"But that'll put us into the backyard."

I nodded. "Exactly where you want to be."

On another occasion, Jean commented she'd always wanted a wet bar but had no space for it. I said, "Oh, yes, there is. See that window over there? Let's take it out and put a bar in its place."

Sometimes, I get the feeling that friends invite me over for the free decorating advice. No matter how often I assure them they have lovely homes, they protest something is lacking, and I say: "If you're really serious . . ."

A few years ago, I actually did turn professional, for a project in Las Vegas called Forest Hills. They asked me to do four model homes. To make them look lived in, I set all the tables with specially selected china, and crystal, and flatware. It didn't take long to learn that people going through the models were sometimes more interested in collecting souvenirs than buying homes. They were ripping off parts of the place settings faster than I could replace them. It finally occurred to me people will steal anything that isn't nailed down, so I siliconed everything to the tables: dishes, glasses, silverware, napkins, everything! The models were sold a little later. The first thing the new owners asked was how to get all this stuff off the tables, and I had to send in a crew with solvents and razor blades.

In spite of the trouble it caused me that one time, I love seeing beautifully set tables. In my own homes, the tables are always set, even if I'm not expecting guests. When I want to get rid of somebody, the settings have a practical purpose. I hate to ask people to leave, but there are some who will stay forever if you don't do something. But they'll look at the table and comment that I must be having guests—perhaps they'd better leave. I've seldom corrected them. With the more persistent ones, I've even added, "Yeah. They'll be here in about thirty minutes."

It always does the trick. Boy, do they fly! With people who know me very well, I sometimes have to say, "Please—I really am having guests tonight!"

Below: The tables are always set chez moi.

NATURE abhors a vacuum, and so do I. That is, the one thing I can't stand is wasted space. I used to have a sun deck on my house in Las Vegas. Because it was too hot in the summer and too cold in the winter, we never used it. I decided to close it in and make an atrium of it, complete with air conditioning and Tivoli lights. I thought it would be fun to make a theme room out of it and decided on a Moroccan motif. The decor, colors, and tiles are all very North African in feeling, and it's turned out very successfully, although it did create a problem for a while.

The room was completed at the same time the newspapers were full of stories about the restaurant I was about to open. People could see the lights of the Moroccan room from the street and assumed that must be the place. They began ringing the bell to ask, "Can you take us without a reservation?"

Once the restaurant was open, we found there was a storeroom we weren't using, and I thought it would make a wonderful private suite for me. There were no windows, and so I used mirrors to reflect light. The front part, which was lit by natural light, flowed back into the apartment, which has an office, a bath, a living room, a kitchen, and a waiting room, in case I'm having a private meeting and there's an overlap with somebody arriving for a later appointment. It's worked out very well. Prior to the doing over of the storeroom, the restaurant staff had to call me at home if they needed me, which meant jumping into a car and racing over there. Now, I can be working there and not be visible if I so choose. I also have a place for business lunches.

With all of my activities, including the restaurant and the museum, which I'll tell you about later in the book, it sometimes seems as if I work so hard on vacation that I have to go back on the road just to get a rest.

CHAPTER 5

All My Children

*I*F somebody were to ask me why a single man needs so many homes, I could reply it's because I have so many children. Twenty-one, to be exact. Five live in Palm Springs but often commute to Los Angeles and Malibu. The rest are in Las Vegas. Before anybody says, "Hey, wait a minute, Liberace's been holding out on us; he's got this big secret family," I'd better explain that my "children" are my dogs. And I couldn't love them more if I'd sired the whole litter. Friends have been known to say "When I die, I want to come back as one of Liberace's dogs."

I won't say I spoil them; it's more the other way around. They spoil me with endless loyalty, love, and fascination. They're all so different, each with his or her own personality. When I travel, I carry framed pictures of them to place around the hotel suites, because I miss them so much. I call home long distance just to speak to them. When they hear the sound of my voice on the phone, they literally go "crazy."

The Palm Springs family consists of two Chinese Shar-peis, Wrinkles and Prunella; a West Highland terrier, Lady Di; a chow, Suzie Wong; and Gretel, a Dutch keeshond. In Las Vegas, I have two Yorkshire terriers, Lady and the Tramp; three Malteses, Charmin', Solo, and Leah; the French poodles Coco, Minuet, Noel, and Snuffy; a cocker spaniel, Blondie; a schnauzer, Precious; a shelty, Lassie; and Chop Suey, a Lhasa apso. There are also three charmers who are "love children": a Lhasa spaniel, Gypsy; a cocker spaniel, Chow

Greeting Andrea McArdle's
ANNIE co-star, Sandy.

Mein; and Southern Comfort, whose lineage is a little of this, and a little of that, and a little of the other thing.

Chow Mein was pushed through my fence, fresh from the groomer, with ribbons in her hair and a prospective litter in her tummy. A note was attached to her collar, asking me to give a good home to "her and hers." When three adorable puppies arrived, I had no trouble placing them among friends and associates. Chow Mein stayed with me, although I did take the precaution of having her spayed. All of my "children" are spayed or neutered for their own protection as well as mine. I'm not ready to be a grandfather yet.

*T*HE first dog in my life was an adorable toy poodle, Suzette, who was shared by my mother and me, when we lived in Sherman Oaks. At that time, Edward R. Murrow's "Person to Person" came to interview me. It was a live television show, for which the cameras came right into your home, while Ed asked questions by remote from his New York studio. We talked about dogs, and I said I loved them, especially poodles.

The next day, I got a call from a woman I didn't know but who lived just a few blocks away. She was moving to New York and had a poodle she couldn't keep because they didn't allow dogs in the apartment she'd taken there. She said she would love to give him to me if I was interested in having him. I asked her to tell me a little about the dog, and she replied, "Well, he's black. And he's the California state champion in obedience."

That was marvelous. I'd have a champion dog. When I drove to her address, the first thing I saw was a great, big chain-link fence around the house. This huge standard poodle bounded over to the fence and climbed up on its hind legs. He was absolutely thrilled to see me. Before I could react, the lady came out and exclaimed, "Oh, it's love at first sight! That dog knows he's found a friend!"

I was looking at this dog, and all I could think was, he's so-o *big*! I asked, "What's his name?"

"Jo-Jo. Don't you love him?"

"Oh, yeah. I love him." I didn't want to hurt the lady's feelings, but what I was really feeling was that when Jo-Jo would see Suzette, he'd eat her.

On the way home, Jo-Jo sat up straight on the front seat next to me, looking as proud as royalty. He seemed to be nodding at the pedestrians and saying, "Look at me. I'm going to live with Liberace."

Below: Lady Di, caught unaware by the photographer.

My mother took one look at Jo-Jo and cried, "Get that beast out of here! He's not a dog, he's a horse!"

I said soothingly, "But, Ma, he's a champion. Look at the tricks he can do."

He sat up on his hind legs, and shook hands, and rolled over, and played dead. Mother still wasn't very keen on him. She said, "We can share Suzette. But that one's all yours!"

When I sold the house in Sherman Oaks, my mother got custody of Suzette, because she was so attached to her. I gave Jo-Jo to my housekeeper, Gladys, who kept him for ten years and thought he was the most devoted and wonderful dog in the world.

*A*S time passed, I began to miss not having a dog. People would say I was crazy to want another pet. I traveled too much. What would I do with it? But the longing wouldn't go away. It was satisfied while I was playing an engagement in San Francisco. Some good friends invited me to supper after the show. Their French poodle had just given birth, and they offered one of the puppies to me. I was so excited when they came into the room, carrying these two absolutely gorgeous balls of fluff, and offered me a choice of male or female. I congratulated the mother on having given birth to two such adorable winners. One of my friends said, "Actually, she had three."

The third was out in the laundry room. They were going to have to put him to sleep, because the vet had said he was so ill it would be better to put him out of his misery as soon as possible. I asked if I might go out to look at the poor thing.

The moment I saw little Baby Boy, it was as if a magnet was drawing me to him. I had to have that puppy. No other would do. I wanted to nurse him back to health, to make him as fine and beautiful as his brother and sister were. I took Baby Boy home with me that very night and, from then on, dedicated myself to making that dog perfect. With the help of much love and nurturing, I succeeded. Baby Boy became my constant and devoted companion. He even took his meals sitting at the table with me.

After Baby Boy, another French poodle, Michi, came into my life. She was brought over by a young lady who couldn't take the dog to work with her. She gave Michi to me on condition that she have visiting rights. At first she came every other day, then once a week and, ultimately, once a month. As the visits became less frequent, Michi's maternal instinct grew, and she began to mother and become very possessive about Baby Boy. It was not long before Michi became totally indifferent to her former mistress, and it was apparent to all of us that she had decided to join the Liberace family.

The family began to grow. It was only later that I started to acquire the pedigreed animals. Most of the dogs I got at the beginning had something wrong with them. They were mixed breeds, or the runts of the litter, or had delicate health. Nobody else wanted them. I guess

Below: Baby Boy, an honored guest at a dinner party.

Above: Lassie at home.

my first reaction is always to reach out to the underdog. In a way, it's like my feeling for houses nobody else sees any virtue in. It's a challenge to turn them into beautiful things filled with love, just as I had done with Baby Boy.

Years later, Baby Boy began to go blind. I made inquiries and discovered there were only three doctors in the county who could perform the operation that would restore his sight. After making the appointments, I got into the car with the dog. He lay very close to me on the seat, seeming to sense I was his best friend. The operation was temporarily successful.

Baby Boy was never a mushy dog. He wasn't the type who leapt on your lap and kissed you or anything like that but, even after he started going blind for the second time, I could walk in the room, and his little tail would wag and he'd begin to quiver. He felt my presence, which made him happy. He was such a pretty fellow that you couldn't tell anything was wrong with him. People were always surprised to learn he couldn't see and was hard of hearing. We babied him and kept him happy and alive for eighteen years.

I'll occasionally be asked how I can spread my affection so thin among so many dogs. It's easy. I love them all, but there are certain dogs that have an intelligence so individual I can't think of them as pets but as people. Baby Boy was like that.

⎯⎯✦⎯⎯

IT'S really incredible to see how much knowledge an animal can absorb. The Shar-peis, Wrinkles and Prunella, are the youngest of my family, but also the most intelligent of the lot. In my opinion, they have vocabularies of twenty to thirty words, which is a lot for dogs. I catch myself spelling because, if I say certain words, they get very excited. For instance, if I say, "Do you want to go for a ride, do you want to go to Malibu?"—they love Malibu—they go crazy.

Malibu Beach is very territorial when it comes to dogs. There are certain areas that seem to belong to certain dogs. I don't want the Shar-peis to go on the beach because they're a fighting breed, and I'm afraid they'll attack the other dogs. They watch them from the balcony. I used to ask, "Are there big dogs today?" They'd go wild, dash all over the apartment, race out on the balcony, run from one end to the other. It's gotten to the point where I don't even use the word "dogs" anymore. They can be lying around, or sound asleep, and all I have to say is, "Let's see if there are any today." They're up in a flash and out on the balcony, peering over to see if there's another dog around. If they should spot one, forget it! They're up on the rails and barking madly as if protecting me from unspeakable dangers.

MY family is tremendous company, always there when I want them, but sensing when I want to be alone and never disturbing me. They also seem to know when I'm busy. If I'm rehearsing at the piano, they'll come and lie under it without trying to jump up, or beg for attention, or make a sound. They're about as attentive an audience as I could ever hope to find.

Below: Gladys catering a dinner party.

The Russian wolfhounds get in the act.

For such a diverse group of breeds, it's amazing how well they get along. It'd be a much better world if that diverse group at the United Nations got along half as well. Mealtime is a show in itself. They respect each other's portions and never steal from one another's bowls.

All my children are very well trained and completely housebroken, thanks to "doggie doors" that are placed in strategic areas throughout the house. The brood that lives in Palm Springs really has the best of it in that respect. My house covers half a block, with Mother's former home right behind it. After Mother passed on, I sold it to some people who have a gift shop in town. We've become very good neighbors, with much visiting back and forth, but it's the dogs who do most of the visiting. Although I've put a gate between the two properties, the dogs just love to go on the other side. In my garden, they have the pool to get around, and a gazebo as well as a wishing well. Over there, they have a straight run, which is what they really love. I only have to say, "Are you ready?" and they're at the door, all set to make a friendly call.

At any of my homes that they happen to be in, they "announce" visitors with their barking. I've even put in musical door chimes that are programmed with seasonal melodies or my theme song, "I'll Be Seeing You," but I can't fool them. They react the same as they did with an ordinary bell. I have one dog, Lady Di, who will try to "sing" whenever I play the piano. The real singer in the family is Julio, a canary who sings up a storm every time I put on one of Julio Iglesias's records.

BECAUSE some of my favorite "children" have been the ones nobody else wanted, I've become a very active member of the Palm Springs Animal Shelter, where they guarantee no animal will be put to sleep, regardless of its age or physical condition. They care for them with medical attention and grooming and try to find them homes.

The shelter started out very small, but now they're moving into a big complex. They have fund-raising drives sponsored by many of the local celebrities, like Bob Hope, Sinatra, and myself. It's so heartwarming to see how many people like and will adopt the animals that nobody else wants. There are so many wonderful pets like Baby Boy, with so much love to give if we'll just open our homes and hearts to them.

Opposite: That's Precious, and she really is!

How "Luckie" Can You Get?

FOR over thirty years, I've been blessed with a housekeeper-cook-friend whom I often refer to as "my Black mother." Her name is Gladys Luckie, and lucky she is. She loves to play the slot machines. When she gets the urge, off she goes, regardless of the house, to one of the casinos. The amazing thing is she always comes home a winner.

I can remember only one time when her luck deserted her. She was sitting at the kitchen table, counting her winnings, and didn't notice a bill falling to the floor. Chow Mein, who loves to chew paper, promptly started to make a feast of it. Before Gladys could get it away from her, the dog had eaten half of what turned out to be a hundred-dollar note.

The next day, I took the half-eaten bill to the bank and was informed no reimbursement could be made, since somebody else might have the other half. I knew who had the other half and was sure it was very well digested by then. Alas, Gladys was out a hundred bucks.

If Gladys has a lucky gambling streak, I've been just as lucky to have found the indispensable Mrs. Luckie. Without her, it would have been impossible to raise all my "children," run all my homes, and still go on working to support them. She is one of my greatest confidantes. I can tell Gladys anything and be sure it will go no further. Because I've become so well known as a collector of objects and

The aptly named Gladys
Luckie.

real estate, I'm always being bothered by people trying to sell me things. I can always put Gladys on the phone with them and be sure she'll politely and firmly get them out of the way.

Gladys was a caterer before coming to work for me. She did parties for people like Louis B. Mayer and Billie Burke, the cream of the Hollywood entertainment world. That's how I first met her. She came to do a large dinner for me.

Her whole family worked for her. She'd gather them all up, and they'd do the marketing, the preparations, the cooking, and the serving, and, what to me is the worst part of any party, the cleaning up—all those dirty dishes, glasses, and caked, stale hors d'oeuvres. You could walk into the kitchen after the last guests had left, and there wouldn't be a sign that there'd ever been a party.

Gladys can cook any kind of food—soul, Italian, Mexican, even Russian. She once went to London to participate in a cook-out with famous chefs from all over, and she won first prize for her beef Stroganoff. I remember asking her if she could do a luau. She told me it was no problem and did the whole thing, including the roast suckling pig.

While Gladys was still in the catering business, her teenage daughters helped as waitresses. At the height of the twist craze, I gave a party and hired a professional dance team to teach us how to do it, but they weren't being very successful. I happened to glance over at one of the daughters, a very pretty girl, who was clearing up and really going to the music. She was so much better than the couple I'd hired that there was no contest. I said, "Forget about those ashtrays. Come over and show us how to do it."

And she did. She was terrific. From then on, whenever I called Gladys to do some catering, I said, "Be sure to bring your daughter. She's the hit of the party."

As Gladys's children got older, they began pursuing their own careers. One became a beautician, another went into show business, and so forth. One day, Gladys came to me and said, "Look, I've raised the kids. They're on their own. Now I'd like to work for you on a steady basis."

I was living in the Hollywood mansion at the time and thought it'd be great to have somebody who could really take over and see that things ran smoothly. This posed a problem for my mother, who had her own wing in the house. It was the idea that somebody was coming who might displace her. She was not used to having servants. She had raised her family and done all of her own cooking and cleaning, and here was this woman twenty years her junior who was going to take over all of those jobs.

Mother tried every which way to get a rise out of Gladys, but Gladys kept her cool. Thank goodness, Gladys is a patient woman and

Below: With Gail Storm and Mom at a party. I succeeded Gail as Mayor of Sherman Oaks.

understood what Mother was going through. To this day, nothing upsets her. She swims with the tide.

The cooking was the first head-on collision. Mother was a good cook but a limited one, strictly a roast chicken, pot roast, and potatoes type. There was nothing Gladys could not do, from the simplest meals to haute cuisine. Often, when I came home from the road, where I'd been lobstered, and prime-ribbed, and steaked to death in fancy restaurants, I'd go into the kitchen and say, "You know what I'd really like tonight? Your meat loaf."

Gladys used to make a great meat loaf. She'd suggest I invite Ray Arnett, my stage manager, and some of his kids over. That made a good party, because Mother liked Ray. One night after the dinner was on the table, my mother turned to him and said, "Arnett"—she always called him by his last name and never his first—"here's my son coming home exhausted from a tour. And what's she fixing for him? A meat loaf!" She nodded toward the kitchen. "You know what they're eating out there? New York steaks!"

To make peace, I began to ask my mother to show Gladys how to make some of the things she used to cook for us when I was a kid. Gladys knew how to prepare these things, but she always let my mother think she was teaching her and, when she served it, she'd announce it was Mother's recipe. At first, Mother would complain it wasn't right, and Gladys would say, "You're absolutely right, Mrs. Liberace. I forgot something. The next time I make it, I want you to watch to make sure it's done correctly."

That Gladys is some diplomat!

· GLADYS'S MEAT LOAF ·

1½ pounds ground chuck beef	4 tablespoons Worcestershire sauce
½ pound veal or ground pork	½ cup chopped parsley
¾ cup bread crumbs	1 egg
⅔ cup chicken broth	1 can Hunts tomato sauce
⅔ cup chopped onions	1 teaspoon Season-All
⅓ cup grated carrots	1 teaspoon garlic salt
⅔ cup chopped red or green pepper	pepper to suit taste

Mix all the ingredients thoroughly, shape into loaf. Mix tomato sauce with can of water, spread evenly over top. Bake 1 hour, 350° oven.

It took a couple of years, but my mother gradually came around on the cooking. The cleaning took a little longer. These were two women who had their own ways of doing things, and they weren't the same. Whenever I phoned to say I was closing that night and would be home the next day, Gladys called in her troops, the people who'd worked for her over the years. There was a mad scramble to deep-clean the whole house: mirrors, windows, floors, chandeliers, upholstery, draperies. If I commented on how spotless everything was, my mother's reply was, "It ought to be. We had the Harlem Globetrotters in here yesterday."

Gladys actually was the peacemaker at home. She'd tip me off in advance when Mom was displeased about one person or another, so that I'd know how to handle the situation when I saw her. One time Gladys took me aside to inform me that Mom had a personal vendetta against our Japanese gardener, who was threatening to quit if she didn't stop harassing him. She'd taken offense at his overuse of the

Opposite: My personal "Queen Mum" on her throne.

hose to sweep away falling leaves and twigs. She'd yell at him from her balcony, "What are you doing, planting rice?"

We tried to reason with Mom, explaining that he was keeping the formal garden very attractive and would be hard to replace. I asked her please not to insult him anymore. She replied, "I didn't insult him. All I said was 'You dirty Jap, get the hell out of here!'"

As time went on, my mother began to mellow and enjoy the comforts of being waited on. Her relationships with the help improved to the point where the gardener never left the premises without leaving a bouquet of freshly cut flowers for her. She began to praise Gladys's cooking and request her favorite dishes. The two became companions and best friends for the rest of my mother's life.

Below: Mom and I breaking ground at Sherman Oaks.

WHEN my mother reached her mid-eighties her health began to fail. On several occasions, my sister, Angie, who was very worried about our mother's condition,

called me on the road to say Mom wasn't going to make it through the night, and I'd better get home. I had to rearrange schedules and charter a plane to get there as fast as I could, only to discover she perked up the moment she saw me. I tried to talk to her about it. The trouble was she wasn't really happy living in Palm Springs, although she had a beautiful home of her own there. She felt lonely. My brother George and his wife were living in Las Vegas. I was playing the Las Vegas Hilton ten or twelve weeks at a time and spending most of my time there. Even Gladys was living in Vegas.

There was one bad scare, when my mother was in the Eisenhower Hospital, and they didn't think she'd make it to morning. I asked, "Mom, what would make you really happy?"

"I'd like to spend my last years in Las Vegas."

"That's no problem. When do you want to move? But you've got to get well first."

I got my first smile of the evening out of her. She said, "Oh, I'll get well. I promise you."

Within twenty-four hours, she was out of the hospital. I rushed back to Vegas to find and furnish a lovely condominium for her. You've never seen a happier woman than Mom during those years she lived in Las Vegas. She loved coming to the Hilton to see me. When other entertainers she liked were playing in town, my sister would take her to their shows. What she hated was the production shows, because of the nudity. When the management asked her opinion, she'd say, "You must've run out of money before you finished the costumes." Those gorgeous costumes with no tops were one thing she couldn't go for.

Most of all, my mother loved going with Gladys to play the slot machines in the hotels where I was appearing. Gladys would periodically come to me for additional playing money when Mom ran out of coins. She'd hit several jackpots but would never put her winnings back in the machines. Why should she? She had her own bank. Me! By the end of the night, her purse was as heavy as if it were nailed to the floor.

Mother was later confined to a wheelchair and a walker, as a result of a broken hip she'd suffered in a fall. When the Hilton Hotel management learned about her accident, they installed several slot machines in my home. How she used to love playing those "one-armed bandits." If she hit a two-hundred-dollar jackpot, and the machine had only twenty dollars in it to drop, the rest had to be paid by the attendant. You've guessed it—I was the attendant.

One afternoon, she won several jackpots, and I owed her over one thousand dollars. I explained I didn't keep that much money around the house, and she replied, "That's all right, son. I'll take a check."

Above: That's lucky me in the middle with Sonja Henie and Susan Hayward.

I really think those machines kept her alive and happy for several extra years. She was eighty-nine when she left us, and I am comforted by the knowledge that her senior years were filled with joy and the greatest attention and love.

Mother's portrait hangs in her favorite room in my Las Vegas house, "the casino," where she spent her happiest hours, playing the slots.

WHEN Gladys decided it was time to retire, I gave her one of my Las Vegas guest houses and a pension. I hired a couple to take her place. Things seemed fine until the first time I had to work on some new material and went up to the second floor to rehearse. Suddenly, there were these two people sitting there and listening. It was "entertain me" time. I get very self-conscious about rehearsing in front of other people, and I got up from the piano. They said, "Oh, you're not going to stop, are you? That sounded so beautiful. We could listen to you for hours."

I tried to explain as nicely as I could that I was rehearsing things that needed work. I made mistakes and didn't like anybody listening to me play anything that wasn't perfect. I promised to let them be my audience as soon as I was ready. They agreed, but I knew it wasn't going to work out. Gladys realized the couple wasn't right for me and changed her mind about retiring. She said, "I've missed the dogs, I've missed the house, and I've missed you. Can I come back?"

We bring in people for all the heavy work, but Gladys is the manager and tells them what to do and how to do it. Although she considers herself sort of in semiretirement, just feeding the dogs is really a full-time job. She keeps a list of their names to make sure she gets around to all of them.

Now that I've got my Tivoli Gardens Restaurant just a few blocks away, I'm seldom home for dinner. When it's only Gladys and I, I usually say, "Don't bother cooking just for me. Let's go over to the restaurant."

It's not just to give her a treat that I invite her over there. She's such a great cook that I value her input on the food we're serving. I ask what she thinks, and she tells me what could be better and what should be done to make it better, which I pass on to the chef.

In my private life, in my homes, in my business, with my family, both canine and human, you can see what I mean about how lucky I was to find Mrs. Luckie.

Opposite: With Mom in the '50s.

The Many Faces of Dorothy

C AN lightning strike twice in the form of good luck with excellent housekeepers who also become treasured friends? It did for me when the irreplaceable Gladys Luckie, who ruled my roosts first in Hollywood and then Las Vegas, was joined by the incomparable Dorothy MacMahain, first in Palm Springs and now wherever she's needed.

Dorothy first came into my life over fifteen years ago, when she was still in her twenties and already the mother of four sons. It was hard to believe, because she looked like little more than a schoolgirl. She wanted to work for a celebrity, and her first choice had been Jerry Lewis, because he was the only one she could think of. I almost lost her the first day. At the time I had a couple and needed Dorothy only as a part-time helper. She lived in Riverside, which meant she would be driving about sixty miles each way to get to work. She later told me her first thoughts were: "I gotta be crazy. I wouldn't do this for anybody. I'm not gonna take this job."

Thank goodness, she had second thoughts. The female half of my couple was the only person I have ever known who could burn soup. Dorothy was so much better than they were that she gradually took over. Now she thinks nothing of driving to my Malibu place, which is as far west of her home as Palm Springs is east, and she takes care of the California places, as well as coming to Las Vegas for special chores.

The more I got to know about Dorothy, the more I admired her. She was one of fifteen children of an itinerant fruit picker. In the summers they lived in tents, and for their weekly bath her father lined up all the

Christmas 1985 in Palm Springs with Dorothy in our holiday sweaters.

kids and sprayed them down with a hose. She was not the oldest, but she looked after all of her sisters and brothers. She married at fifteen and had four sons of her own. I call her Mother Goose, because she's such a baby lover. She can't resist a pregnant woman. She rushes up to them to ask how they're feeling, and when the baby's due, and do they want a boy or girl. When her daughters-in-law are having babies, she drops whatever she's doing to rush over to be with them. She just loves to take charge and look after people. Some of her sisters are good helpers, but they're not leaders. Our Dorothy is a leader.

In her forties, she still looks like she's in her twenties. She's beautiful and extremely feminine, but she's capable of doing the work of four men. Besides keeping my homes immaculate, she can housepaint, garden, wash cars, cook, and serve guests, always looking lovely in an attractive uniform. She does all of this and never loses her wonderful disposition; she's always smiling and happy, with a marvelous sense of humor.

Dorothy never got beyond the eighth grade, and there's one thing that gives her problems. Spelling. She spells phonetically, which can sometimes cause problems when she goes marketing for me. One night, I was having a small dinner party and thought a chateaubriand would make a good main course. I sent Dorothy down to the store to pick one up, along with a few other things. Off she dashed, not letting on that she'd never heard of chateaubriand.

She raced up and down the aisles, studying all the packages of meat and looking for a something with a label remotely like what she'd spelled on her list. In desperation, she finally called over the butcher. Peering at her list, she said, "I'm looking for a something—you know—a chauteau—something or other."

"Do you mean a chateaubriand?" She snapped her fingers and smiled. "That's it."

He told her he'd make one up while she finished her shopping. I'd also asked her to pick up some Dubonnet, because some of my guests preferred aperitifs to cocktails.

While I was cooking, I asked Dorothy to fix me a Dubonnet on the rocks. She opened the bottle and brought me some. I tasted it and asked, "What is this? It sure doesn't taste like Dubonnet."

I looked at the bottle. It was Drambuie. Dorothy shrugged. "Well, I got the first letter right, didn't I?"

We both laughed. Her spelling is something about which she good-naturedly takes a lot of kidding. But I have to say this for Dorothy, she's the quickest study I know. You have to show her how to do something only once. She'll never be the cook Gladys is, but all she has to do is watch me prepare a dish one time, and the next time she'll be able to make it for me perfectly.

Y the time Dorothy came into our lives, my mother had learned how to get along with servants. Mother was clean-crazy, one of those people who was constantly polishing and dusting, and she loved Dorothy, because Dorothy was clean-crazy, too. If I want to make her happy, all I have to do is buy her a new cleaning product.

One of Dorothy's big passions is polishing silver. In my Hollywood penthouse, I have a table in the living room with a collection of antique silver. I can look at it and be pleased with how beautiful it is. All Dorothy sees is tarnish. She'll never ask me about it, but the next time I pass the table, it'll be cleared off. She'll be out in the kitchen, polishing away. I'll say, "Are you deep-cleaning again?"

"I couldn't stand looking at this silver another minute. It's turning gold, and it's not what-cha-ma-call-it."

"Vermeil."

"Right."

There was one time when my collector-crazy outmatched her clean-crazy. I love antique silver. If I see something really fine in a

Below: I can't remember now if I bought out the whole store, but I'll bet I came pretty close.

shop, I have to have it. I was unpacking some new pieces when she came into the room. She took one look and cried, "You bring one more piece of silver in here, and I'm gonna quit!"

But I noticed that, at the same time she was complaining, she was compulsively reaching for the silver polish.

Above: The multi-talented Dorothy in the garden.

*G*ARDENERS have to work every day of the year to make the desert of Palm Springs bloom. Dorothy has a green thumb as good as any of theirs. There are flowers everywhere you look, all of which she planted. She's really Dame Nature as well as Mother Goose.

My Palm Springs home, which I call The Cloisters, without Dorothy would never run as well as it does. She takes as much pride in it as I do. All of her mothering instincts come out with my Palm Springs "children." She loves the dogs, and they love her. She doesn't even mind when I kid her about being a "super-duper pooper scooper."

WHEN I say Dorothy is not only a fabulous housekeeper but also my devoted friend, I mean it from the bottom of my heart. On occasion, she'll get all decked out in her best dress and attend an opening night or a festive dinner as my "date." She looks so glamorous that people think she must be some television or motion picture star. She's as pretty as any of them and prettier than most. Actually, she looks quite a bit like Linda Evans, of "Dynasty" fame.

One very special Hollywood event last year was the Variety Clubs benefit Frank Sinatra was hosting in honor of President and Mrs. Ronald Reagan. Everybody who was anybody wanted to be there. When I told Dorothy I was taking her, she was absolutely flabbergasted. She said, "Oh, I don't want to embarrass you."

I replied, "Dorothy, how could you possibly embarrass me?" She had two short teeth, which made her very self-conscious. I sent her to my dentist, who fitted her with a couple of crowns, and her mouth looked fabulous. Once that was attended to, the next question was what we should wear. It was a formal affair, and we could be sure everybody was going to be in their very best "drop dead" outfits.

In Hollywood, with all of its fabulous shops, it wasn't hard to find a very pretty dress for a very pretty girl like Dorothy. As for myself, I never wear a black tuxedo when it says "black tie." Maybe that's because I don't want anybody to think I rented it. I thought I had the perfect dinner suit. It never occurred to me it wasn't in Hollywood. I hate to pack and unpack, so I keep complete wardrobes in each of my homes. That must sound strange, coming from somebody who spends as much time on the road as I do, but, believe me, if I had to do my own packing and unpacking, I'd quit show business.

For this very important evening, I slipped up. The clothes I wanted to wear were in Las Vegas. Instead of bothering to send for them, I just went out and bought a whole new outfit. Well, what else would you expect Liberace to do? As everybody knows, I'm a world-class shopper.

When I say this was a very special evening, I mean it was unique right down to locale. It was held at the NBC studios in Burbank, even though it was being filmed for a CBS special. Frank Sinatra must be very close to the President, because I don't think he'd have appeared for anybody else, even though the Variety Clubs were naming a children's hospital in his honor. There were over one hundred children from all over the world, dressed in the costumes of their native countries. President and Mrs. Reagan took the time and effort to shake hands with each and every one of those youngsters. It was very moving.

It was a glorious evening, filled with glorious entertainment, but

Opposite: I haven't got a thing to wear.

Above: As you can see, I really do support the Austrian rhinestone business.

they didn't let you forget it was a television show. As with all other filmed television shows, there would be countdowns. If somebody goofed their lines, they had to reshoot. The guests were told not to look at the cameras, to laugh and not hold it in if they heard something funny, to remember their cues, and so forth. I thought it was amazing to see the President and the First Lady of the United States getting all these instructions from a television director and being such good sports about it.

Dorothy spent the evening saying, "Who's that over there? I know her. I've seen her on TV. What's her name?" Then, we'd run down the roster of stars in her favorite shows for identification. When she did recognize somebody, like all the rest of us fans, she was wrong as often as she was right.

We were seated at a table filled with very well-known and distinguished people. Dorothy whispered, "I know that guy, but I can't place him."

"Which one?"

"Sitting right across from you. He does commercials."

"Oh, you mean Cliff Robertson."

Cliff asked who she was and what she did. Dorothy replied very grandly, "I'm Liberace's Girl Friday, Saturday, and Sunday, Monday, Tuesday, Wednesday, and Thursday, too."

When we got home later and turned on the television, there was Cliff Robertson selling AT&T. Dorothy got so excited. She kept exclaiming, "I had dinner with him!"

After the show was over, people started getting up from their tables and gathering around the President. It was a real mob scene, which was very unusual. These days, you never see the President without secret-service men surrounding him. If there was any security that night, it was very loose. I said to Dorothy, "Wouldn't it be wonderful to go over and say hello to the President? And shake hands? But I'm a little reluctant to join the mob. Let's wait until it thins out a little bit."

While we were waiting, Dorothy said, "You think I should remind President Reagan that I once served him dinner?"

I looked at her quizzically, and she continued, "It's true. I was working as a waitress at a party given by the Justin Darts, and he was there."

Before she retired, Mrs. Dart was the actress Jane Bryan. Ronald Reagan and she started their careers at the same time at Warner Brothers. It only proves show business is a small world. Almost as small as politics.

Dinner was about to be served, and the crowd was dispersing, and I decided it was time for Dorothy to meet the President without a tray in her hands. He couldn't have been more charming or pleasant. Dorothy didn't believe what was happening to her. While she was shaking his hand, I could feel her whole body trembling. The President and she were a study in contrasts. He was so relaxed, and she was so thrilled.

Below: With Rick James.

I'VE been so fortunate to have people around me that I love and who appreciate beautiful things as much as I appreciate them—Dorothy for fifteen years and Gladys for over thirty. It sometimes makes me think I must be doing something right.

Right: President Reagan giving Dorothy
one of her most unforgettable moments.

Liberace Cooks

*I*N all of my homes, my favorite room is the kitchen. I love open kitchens or, at least, kitchens with sitting areas. For one thing, I don't think the chef should be penalized for preparing the dinner by being isolated from his guests. People also enjoy watching to see how certain dishes are prepared.

When I'm doing an informal dinner party, I don't mind if the cooking turns into a communal affair. Invariably, somebody will say they make the greatest such and such dish, and I'll tell them, "Be my guest." That's especially true with salads. They just love to mix salads, and I've usually got all the ingredients. If I've been in residence in any of my homes for more than a day or two, you can be sure I've stocked the refrigerator with all kinds of fresh greens, vegetables, and fruits.

I love to cook. I must have inherited my interest in the culinary arts from my Italian father and Polish mother. Without knowing it, they were both gourmet cooks in the cuisine of their homelands and passed on to their children an appreciation of international cuisine.

In high school, I inaugurated a chef's course that became very popular with my fellow students. They not only learned how to prepare foods but also how to recognize various cuts of meat and poultry, select the freshest produce, plan menus, and create interesting place settings. In my opinion, a pretty-looking table is as important to the enjoyment of a good meal as the things that are served on it.

The culmination of the course was a father and son banquet. All twenty-six students were graded on the contributions they made to

Even in the kitchen I am
never far from a keyboard.

Above: My version of a piano bar.

the dinner. Every course, from appetizer to dessert, was accompanied (for the fathers only) by an appropriate wine. It took a little persuasion on my part to get permission for the wines to be brought into school. But it was after regular classes were over, and none of the proud fathers overindulged.

I remember the time all of us decided to bake Christmas fruitcakes. To save time in class, we chopped the citrons, candied fruits, and nuts at home. Somehow, when we were finished, my fruitcakes tasted so much better than the others that I was encouraged to make additional cakes for Christmas gifts. It was then that my mother told me about her secret ingredient. The night before I'd taken the chopped fruits and nuts to school, she'd soaked them in brandy.

Since then, I've enjoyed many wonderful experiences in the kitchen. Most of my meals have been received with pleasure by my guests, but one in Palm Springs turned into a disaster. I'd decided to make my Liberace Lasagna, which was always a special favorite with my friends.

The aroma of two large pans baking in the oven was increasing appetites by the minute. At the last moment, I decided an extra sprinkle of Parmesan cheese would enhance the flavor. I reached for the green-and-red foil can of grated cheese but, in my haste, accidentally grabbed the look-alike can of Comet, which was also on the counter top. Needless to say, I ruined both pans of lasagna before noticing that the surfaces were turning blue from the cleanser.

Imagine my embarrassment when I had to admit what I'd done to twelve hungry guests, which is the same number as the members of a jury in court. They certainly passed sentence when they had to settle for take-out Kentucky fried chicken (with eleven secret herbs and spices added). By the way, I've switched to Ajax, the foaming cleanser with a different-colored can. I also now freshly grate my cheese, which improves the taste in more ways than one.

Here is that famous Liberace Lasagna recipe, minus, of course, the Comet.

· LIBERACE LASAGNA ·
(Serves eight)

2 tablespoons and one teaspoon olive oil

1 cup minced onions

2 cloves garlic, chopped

1 large can peeled, chopped Italian tomatoes

1 small can tomato paste

3 tablespoons minced fresh parsley

1 tablespoon minced fresh basil (or ¹/₂ teaspoon dried)

1 teaspoon Italian herbs (or spices)

¹/₂ cup water

4 Italian sausages

1 8-ounce package of lasagna noodles

1 egg yolk

1 small carton ricotta cheese

1 package mozzarella cheese

¹/₂ cup Parmesan or Romano cheese, grated (or a combination of both)

1. Heat 2 tablespoons of olive oil in a saucepan.
2. Sauté the onions and garlic until they turn translucent but not brown.
3. Add the tomatoes, tomato paste, parsley, basil, herbs or spices, and water. Bring the ingredients to a boil and then simmer on medium heat for at least two hours, until the sauce takes on a smooth consistency. (Shortcut: Eliminate steps 1–3 and substitute a large jar of your favorite brand of prepared Italian marinara sauce.)
4. Preheat oven to 300° F.
5. Broil the sausage, drain off the excess fat, and slice thin.
6. Begin to prepare the lasagna noodles according to the instructions on

the label. Add 1 teaspoon of olive oil to prevent sticking. Do not boil the noodles for the full time but only until they are flexible, just before the *al dente* stage.

7. Drain the noodles in a colander and add ice cubes for quick cooling and easier handling.

8. Stir the egg yolk into the ricotta cheese.

9. In a 9 by 11-inch baking dish, alternate the layers of lasagna with sauce, mozzarella, ricotta, Parmesan or Romano cheese, and sausage. The top layers should be cheese.

10. Bake for 45 minutes, until the noodles are tender and the sauce is bubbling. Just before serving, add an additional sprinkling of Parmesan cheese (*not* Comet).

This recipe serves eight generously. I usually prepare a double recipe and freeze one dish without baking it. You don't have to defrost it before baking, but it takes twice the time in the oven (approximately 1 1/2 hours) for the noodles to get tender and the sauce to bubble.

I HAVE one rule of thumb about cooking: if you can read, you can cook. It doesn't take much skill or experience to follow a recipe. All it takes is a measuring cup and the patience to do exactly what the instructions dictate. Later, as you gain experience and develop your own style and tastes, you can make changes, adding things you think would be good, replacing one ingredient with another you like better. But at the beginning, it's not a good idea to try to improve on the expert who wrote the book.

There are more and more products coming on the market that provide wonderful shortcuts, and I think it's ridiculous not to take advantage of them. All of us are capable of foolish mistakes in the kitchen, but these products are foolproof. If you start to bake a cake from scratch, a telephone call at the wrong moment can ruin the whole recipe. The cake mixes by people like Duncan Hines and Betty Crocker have been perfected by master chefs and are as good as most things coming out of the fanciest bakeries. If you follow the instructions on the packages, there's no way you can go wrong, and it's usually possible to add a touch that makes the recipes your own. If they call for margarine, I'll use sweet butter. I may throw in two eggs for one or add some chopped nuts or rum.

Is there anything worse than lumpy mashed potatoes? That's the

Opposite: The oven in the armoire.
Overleaf: This time I really am
expecting guests.

way they often turn out when you start from scratch, because this deceptively simple vegetable dish is much harder to do right than it seems. The potatoes have to be cooked for exactly the right time or they fall apart or get waterlogged. The mashing takes a lot of time and even more elbow grease. You just can't beat the instant mashed potatoes. They're quick and always just right. They're even made from the best Idaho potatoes and provide a variety of dishes. For that personal touch, add a little extra butter, chopped chives, parsley or dill, some grated cheese, or gravy.

I've had people say, "If you're going to cook dinner for me, I hope it's not going to come out of a jar or package."

I say, "Oh, no," and do my little magic with the potatoes and the cake mix. When my guests have finished dining, they come away raving about the meal.

Of course, there are things that can't be improved upon by shortcuts. They take the touch of a master chef. Gladys's fried chicken is an example and a half. Gladys makes the world's best fried chicken. For years, I watched her and tried to copy it, but it never tasted the same. It was good but not the same. I'd say to myself, "I know she's doing something and keeping it from me. When I turn my head, she puts something else in there I don't know about."

I'd question her, and she'd always say, "I just put salt and pepper on it and fry it."

"What do you fry it in?"

"A little bit of this and a little bit of that."

Once I caught her reaching under the counter where she kept some drippings. I thought—oh, that's the secret! I tried it, but all I tasted was the drippings. Some great cooks are like that. They just know and no matter how much they want to, can't tell you what they do. Of course, some are just evasive. It's like the old story of the Hungarian cook who was asked how she made her wonderful chicken paprikash and she replied, "First, you steal a chicken."

I think I can finally do the fried chicken almost as well as Gladys does it. When I entertained my young friend Michael Jackson, I thought I'd surprise him with a real Southern soul-food meal, including the chicken and other recipes Gladys had taught me. On the way into the dining room, Michael said, "Oh, I forgot to tell you—I'm a vegetarian."

Thank God for the fresh produce and frozen vegetables I always keep on hand. A vegetarian dish was created in a matter of minutes, but vegetables are pretty bland all by themselves. A Hollandaise sauce to accompany them would really help, but it would take a long time to make, and there was no guarantee it wouldn't curdle. Here was an example of how those new shortcut products can save the day.

At the supermarket, I'd bought a package of instant Hollandaise sauce, made from a prize-winning recipe. A little stirring, a little water, a little heating, and it became the greatest Hollandaise I'd ever tasted, and I'd sampled it in some of the world's best restaurants.

J'VE done so many kitchens in so many different homes that I've learned what is necessary and what is superfluous. One important lesson was trying to resist the lure of the gadgets. I've got to admit, I'm a pushover for them. When I first started outfitting kitchens, I had to have every one in sight. The moment the Cuisinart came on the market, I couldn't wait to get one. Somehow,

the directions got misplaced. I plugged it in and tried every which way to get that thing to work and—no way! I took it back to the store and said, "I think I have a faulty one."

The salesman plugged it in, gave a little twist to the top, and it worked perfectly. I felt so ridiculous, and sheepishly walked out with my machine under my arm. I used it a few times, but mostly it sits on the shelf. Now I have Oscar, which is a small version of the Cuisinart that I couldn't wait to get. I've used that a few times, too. The counter is cluttered with appliances that are all great. The problem is I have to be reminded to use them.

I guess I'm a little bit like the European chefs. I chop by hand, and I grate by hand, and I whisk by hand. They say a pianist's hands are his professional fortune. In the service of preparing a good meal, mine have been blistered while frying, scraped while grating, burned while getting something out of the oven, and cut while chopping, and they still work pretty well at the keyboard.

Consistency is the secret of a recipe, and most of the time you can't really control it with a gadget. If you don't watch out, things are pureed instead of chopped, and all the air is beaten out of egg dishes that should be light and fluffy. I know gadgets are supposed to save time, but did you ever count up all the time that's wasted cleaning them and putting them away, to say nothing of shifting them around so there's enough room on the counter for the food?

———※———

ONE of the greatest pleasures of my worldwide tours is the chance to explore the cuisines of so many countries. I've met so many hospitable people eager to take me to the best restaurants in their respective hometowns. What I enjoy most is going off to do some gastronomical exploring by myself and finding the little out-of-the-way places where the local people dine. When I find a bistro that looks interesting, I go in, order a glass of wine, and look around at what everybody's eating. If it looks good, I tell the waiter, "You know, I'm a little hungry, after all. Let me see the menu."

I usually end up having a wonderful dinner of local dishes prepared to order. A few times, I've had to pay for my adventuresomeness. I remember a café in Montmartre I couldn't resist, because it looked so quaint and charming. The next morning, I came down with a not so quaint and charming case of ptomaine poisoning.

I'm always fascinated by the different styles of architecture and design of the restaurants I've encountered in my travels. Visiting the

Tivoli Gardens, in Copenhagen, was an unforgettable experience, a wonderland of twinkling lights with about seventeen restaurants on the grounds, all serving different cuisines. I remember thinking idly that I'd like to have a place of my own just like it but never dreaming at the time that I, indeed, soon would have my own Tivoli Gardens.

After I opened my first museum in Las Vegas (more about that later), I discovered that the bus drivers were taking the people on the museum tour to a very mediocre cafeteria for lunch. It didn't seem right. I thought I might open a kind of elegant cafeteria next to the museum, featuring good food served quickly. Before I could do anything about it, a brand-new, huge cafeteria opened across the street. I

Opposite: Easter Sunday at the Beverly Wilshire Hotel.
Below: Checking the table before an intimate dinner party in my Hollywood den.

Left: What makes you think this is the
Palm Springs garage?

thought I couldn't compete with it unless I did something different and beyond it. Before I knew what was happening, what started out to be a nice lunchroom for the convenience of museum visitors evolved into a Liberace production number of a gourmet restaurant. The main restaurant seats one hundred fifty but, when combined with the other rooms, the place seats three hundred. It was a big undertaking, which merited the name I gave it, Tivoli Gardens.

The restaurant has what I call "theme" rooms. The English Room, with a bar, is not a typical London pub. It's based on the magnificent dining rooms found in the country inns that were once great estates. It's the most expensive room in the restaurant. The dark, reddish mahogany moldings and architectural details are all magnificently carved. While I was planning it, everybody around me asked if I was sure I wanted to go that far. It would cost a small fortune. I shrugged. "If I'm going to do it, I'm going to do it right."

The piano lounge was very easy to create, because it was like creating a costume. It's full of twinkling lights, and crystals and mirrors with my theme song engraved around the edges. It not only has the world's largest piano bar but also a mirrored piano that plays electronically as well as manually.

I've always loved swans and I indulged my affinity for them in the Swan Room. All of the decor, artifacts, and pictures relate the theme of the swan.

The Orchid Room is in memory of my mother, who once had an orchid named after her. The flowers, walls, fabrics, and the entire room are done in shades of the color orchid.

The ballroom is very French, with Louis XIV furniture, crystal chandeliers, and great sweeps of drapery. The Antique Room is in about ten different periods. Depending on the diner's mood, the setting can be Oriental, Italian, or almost anything that strikes his fancy. I even have one setting I think of as presidential, because it suggests something that could be found in the White House. All of these things come from my personal collection. If anybody falls in love with and wants to buy the furniture and dishes, the dinner is on the house. It sounds crazy, but I'm constantly replacing the settings that have been purchased by some of my more affluent customers.

When we first opened, I thought you created an attractive ambience and served good food and that's all there was to running a successful restaurant. I soon learned better. I was creating my dream Tivoli Gardens with all of the lavishness of a show-business spectacle. Everything had to be the finest. There was gold-plated flatware, and special china with my logo on it. Service plates that cost over forty dollars apiece. It was a souvenir hunter's paradise. And did they hunt! It was more like big-game hunting. They even took the crystals off the

Opposite: Guess who's in the kitchen with Mom?

Above: The glittering duo—Debbie
Reynolds and me.

chandeliers. They had to be replaced within two months. As for ashtrays—well, I've just given up on ashtrays. If there were as many smokers as there were ashtray swipers, the Surgeon General would kill himself.

THE chefs all know I'm considered a good cook. They're always asking for the recipes for the meals I serve at home, especially at the holidays. The day before our first Thanksgiving at the Tivoli Gardens, I went in to cook the Liberace Thanksgiving dinner for all the chefs and head waiters. I did a dinner for a dozen people, just like the one I was serving the next day at home. I did all the chopping, and mixing, and blending by hand. They thought it was marvelous and exactly what they wanted to duplicate for the holiday special dinner. They made notations on the recipes for the turkey dressing and other dishes, and then did the ordering of the ingredients.

The next day, something told me I'd better go around before the customers started to arrive, to see how they were doing. I hadn't taken one thing into consideration. Because a restaurant serves so many people, there is heavy-duty equipment to do all the things I did by hand. It was gadget time all over again, only on a very large scale.

One of the first things I saw in the kitchen was this giant vat filled with something that was being churned. I tasted it and asked, "What's this?"

"Why, that's your mother's dressing."

"No, it isn't. My mother's dressing is lumpy. It's got consistency. This is like sausage meat. I never meant for it to be beaten to death. You've got to do it by hand like I do."

We had to put in an emergency call to our suppliers to get more ingredients, which would give it a homemade feeling. I went down the line to sample the whole dinner. Everything had been done in such large quantities that they hadn't taken the time to add a pinch of this, a pinch of that, or a few drops of the other thing. The whole box went in. One of the dishes was a baked, candied squash, which I do with brown sugar and butter. Just before serving, I add a few drops of brandy and put it under the broiler to flame it. When I sampled what they had done, it tasted like you needed a chaser. There was so much brandy in it that the squash had completely lost its identity. I asked, "How did you do that?"

"Oh, we used three bottles of brandy."

"My God," I said. "That's enough brandy to sink a battleship."

Fortunately, we caught the mistakes in time, or they would've ruined everybody's holiday. From then on I paid close attention to any recipe I gave them and always said, "Please, don't make it any differently, or it won't come out the way it should."

I'M never going to make any fortunes on the Tivoli Gardens. It costs too much to keep it up to the high standards I've set for it. But it's given so many people, including me, so much pleasure, that it's been worth it. When King Carl XVI Gustaf, of Sweden, visited Las Vegas, his aides chose the Antique Room in my restaurant for a special luncheon in his honor, to which I was invited. The next day the media, which covered the royal event, said, "The food was indeed fit for a king."

Below: Tapping my resources in the Hollywood playroom.

The Month of Christmas

*D*ECEMBER is my favorite month of the year, because it's the month of Christmas. No matter how poor we were when I was growing up, we managed to have a wonderful Christmas, and so it's always been a very special time for me. The tinsel, the glitter, the lights, the decorations: it's almost as if the whole world has become a fantastic, month-long production number. Everybody seems filled with love and in such high spirits. During that season, you can really believe there's peace on earth and good will toward men.

In a way, Christmas is all year 'round for me. Wherever my tours take me, I'm always on the lookout for things that will make wonderful presents. I always plan for the holiday well in advance. The first thing I do is take a shopping trip through my Las Vegas Christmas present warehouse, where I store all those gifts I've accumulated during my trips around the country and the world.

For the man or woman who supposedly has everything, I can always find the most unusual, one-of-a-kind gift right in the warehouse. I'm very careful about my selections for my family, close friends, associates, and employees. The rule is I give only those things I'd love to receive myself.

I live in so many different worlds and so many different places that one Christmas party is never enough. My first party is held early in the month, in the ballroom of the Tivoli Gardens Restaurant. It's for all of my Las Vegas friends and employees. I personally take charge of

Mom and me during
Christmas in the '50s.

128

supervising the dinner, which will be repeated by the chefs later in the month for the restaurant clientele.

The restaurant party is very festive. There are special presents for all of the guests: everything from watches and jewelry to gourmet food baskets for those with families. Fellow performers will often perform, but it has to be because they want to, not because they feel it's expected of them. One year, Dolly Parton sang several songs. She even brought her accompanist and back-up singers. I love that lady and her marvelous talent. Her version of "Winter Wonderland" gives me goose bumps and a happy emotional charge. Dolly's Christmas album with Kenny Rogers is one of my favorites and is played in all my homes during the holidays. Kenny and she make a perfect pair.

My next party is held in my Hollywood penthouse. Most of the guests are my friends in the entertainment industry. All of the Christmas trees are decorated with twinkling lights and fresh-cut flowers. There's a tree in every one of the ten rooms, and each one has different flowers—everything hung in little glass tubes filled with water, so they will last for three or four days, which is all the time I have to spend there during that season. The terrace of the penthouse is like

Below: With my friends Cary James and Kenny Rogers.
Opposite: Playing Santa Claus with Mom in her later years.

Christmas all year 'round. It is permanently adorned with twinkling Tivoli lights. Ceramic birds set in the wall spray little streams of water into the blue-lit swimming pool.

It seems as if the Hollywood party is barely over before I'm off to Malibu. My condo is so close to the ocean that it's almost like a party on a cruise ship. The focal point of the beach decorations is a black-lacquered Christmas tree adorned with crystal ornaments and tiny mirrors that reflect a starburst of colors even in the daylight.

The Malibu party is a neighborhood affair, and the guests include people who live nearby, like Shirley MacLaine and Isabel Sanford (of "The Jeffersons" television fame), as well as some of the soap-opera stars who've become new friends, like Linda Dano (Felicia Gillant in "Another World").

Opposite: Lucky me with Dolly Parton.
Above: Dining with my favorite soap
opera star Linda Dano.

𝒯HE most personal of my Christmas parties is the family reunion in Palm Springs. That one is for my sister, Angie, her two children, Diane and Fred, three grandchildren, and my show-business family, who've been with me for many years. They can choose from the guest rooms, each of which has a different decorative motif. The art in the Gloria Vanderbilt Suite includes the Liberace memorabilia collage that Miss Vanderbilt created especially

for me and presented to me on the "Mike Douglas Show." The Valentino Room features the sleigh bed from Falcon's Lair, the legendary star's Hollywood home. There is also a Zebra Room and, off the pool, the Persian Tent Room. For extra guests, I reserve nearby private villas, which are decorated with Christmas poinsettias in advance of their arrival. They'll also find personal terry-cloth robes and slippers, which they can take home with them when they leave, as well as the Liberace sandalwood soaps that are in the shape of pianos.

Last year, we were sixteen when we sat down to dinner. I don't like large parties. When I first started on television, I was more or less coerced, for my career, into giving mammoth affairs, which I never enjoyed. My idea of a good party is one where I'm able to converse with my guests.

I try to cook things that can be done in advance and need only a few extra minutes to get on the table. The preparing starts long before the meal. Dorothy and some of the others help with the chopping and cutting, and it's like a pre-party party.

Before dinner, the choir of the Church of Our Lady of Solitude sings carols in the garden of The Cloister (that's the name of my house), and a priest says Mass in my Saint Anthony shrine. Saint Anthony has been my favorite saint since a time when everybody thought I was going to die in the Saint Francis Hospital, in Pittsburgh. A very young and lovely nun, wearing a white habit, came to see me late one night, when I was very near death. She said she was going to pray to Saint Anthony for me, and he would make me well. The very next day, I began to get well. I described my nun to the

Below: Christmas in Palm Springs.

Mother Superior at the hospital and asked who she was. The Mother Superior replied, "There are no nuns in this hospital who wear white habits."

I've always been indebted to the Saint Francis Hospital and have kept in touch with the staff. They're going to build a very glamorous, new entrance. It's going to be called the Liberace Entrance, because I'm their best-known patient. In the lobby, there'll be a piano and a large photograph of me. It's one of the nicest things that's ever happened to me.

Ever since the experience at Saint Francis, I've been drawn to anything connected with Saint Anthony. I started collecting religious artifacts, relics, even a stained-glass window and, when I redid The Cloister, I built a shrine in his honor. The statue of Saint Anthony came from Italy and was coated with layers of paint and years of grime. I cleaned it up and discovered it was a wood carving dating to the sixteenth century. Saint Anthony has always been very good to me. I don't think of him as my patron but as my special friend.

At dinner, everybody takes turns making a short toast. We reminisce about old friends and loved ones and Christmases past. Soon, we find we're smiling through our tears.

Left: On safari in Palm Springs.

Each year, our feast is slightly different from the previous one. The one thing that's always included is my Liberace Sticky Buns, because they're such a favorite with all of my guests. Last year, we started with an international fresh-fruit sorbet. It's called international because all of the fruits are imported and out of season. There are things like passion fruit, which you can't find in the stores, as well as other exotic ingredients which come from as far away as New Zealand and Hawaii. I have a friend who makes Italian sorbets out of all these fruits.

We followed with turkey, with my mother's dressing, and all of the unusual condiments I associate with the holiday, such as pickled peaches, and pears, and crab apples. After a feast like that, dessert is superfluous, so we adjourn to the room with the trees and the presents. There's coffee and after-dinner drinks, as well as fruitcake, cookies, and nibbles for anybody with a craving for sweets. It's a very traditional family get-together.

I thought you might like the recipe for my Liberace Sticky Buns.

· LIBERACE STICKY BUNS ·
(18 Buns)

1 cup white raisins	1/4 teaspoon each of ground nutmeg, allspice, cloves, and ginger
3/4 cup light rum	
1 1/2 cups brown sugar	3 packages (18 buns) Pillsbury crescent dough
1/2 pound (two sticks) unsalted butter	1 cup chopped pecans
1/2 teaspoon cinnamon	1 cup whole pecans
	Butter for greasing pans

1. Soak the raisins in the rum over a low flame. Set aside.
2. Preheat oven to 325°F.
3. In a saucepan, melt the butter and stir in the spices and the brown sugar until the mixture becomes a bubbling syrup.
4. Unroll the crescent dough, keeping each package in one flat place.
5. Drizzle one quarter of the syrup over each individual piece of dough, reserving the last one quarter for later.
6. Sprinkle one third of the raisins and spread one third of the chopped pecans on each of the three sheets of dough.
7. Roll up each section of dough, jelly-roll style, and cut into 1-inch pieces.
8. Grease two eight-muffin pans or three six-muffin pans with butter.
9. Put a scant teaspoon of the reserved syrup and a few whole pecans in the bottom of each muffin mold. Cover with the individual jelly-roll pieces, cut side up.

10. Bake in the preheated oven for the time recommended on the Pillsbury packages.
11. While the pans are still hot, invert them on a sheet of heavy aluminum foil, allowing the buns to be released. Replace any of the syrup and pecans that cling to the molds on the individual buns.

You should serve my sticky buns while they're still warm and have that fresh-from-the-oven taste. Believe me, there'll be none left over.

---

*A*FTER dinner, the moment arrives that the children in all of us have been waiting for. It's time to open the presents, a joyous rite that goes on for hours. I love to prolong the suspense and anticipation, by opening mine last. There's

Below: My table for the family Christmas party in Palm Springs.

a lot of picture-taking, including video tapes with sound. Not only do they make nostalgic keepsakes, but they're a good record of who gave what to whom, which prevents repeats of the same gift the following year. Alas, that's happened more than once in the past.

In recent years, my Christmases have become very personal. I used to spend a great deal of money sending out as many as five hundred "trade gifts" each December. One year, I used a professional gift-wrapping service. I gave very explicit instructions, for the ladies' gifts to be wrapped in gold paper and the men's in silver paper. Obviously, I wasn't explicit enough, because all the ladies received cuff links, while the men got earrings.

You can be sure I received a lot of "peculiar" thank-you notes, including one from a prominent television executive, accompanied by a photograph of him wearing his earrings. Nowadays, no one would be surprised, since women are wearing men's shirts, and some men, at least, are wearing one earring. I guess I was just ahead of my time.

I also used to send out a minimum of six thousand specially designed and elaborate Christmas cards, which including postage cost thousands of dollars.

These "trade gifts" have very little to do with real sentiment and a lot to do with business. They go back to the days of the all-powerful columnists, when Louella Parsons and Hedda Hopper would call individual stars and place orders for what they wanted for Christmas. If anybody dared not send it, he was "dead" in the columns.

I've found a better thing to do with the money. Now, I send a simple card with the message that the expenditure is being donated to my foundation in their names. Through the Liberace Foundation, we've set up scholarships at universities across the country for a minimum of ten thousand dollars each. We choose schools that need financial help in their scholarships programs, rather than places like New York's Juilliard, which are self-supporting.

The recipients are not chosen by me but by the schools themselves, and are based on talent, need, and scholarship. We started with seven universities and are now up to twenty-one. At first, scholarships were given only to students in the musical performing arts: pianists, various other instrumentalists, and singers. We're broadening to include the dance and art world, so that the program covers the creative as well as the performing arts. I want to reiterate that I have nothing to do with the selection of the winners. If you are or know a worthy student, you have to contact a university in your area rather than me.

One of my great pleasures on tour is meeting these young people and their teachers. Occasionally, I'll ask one of them to play during my show. The warmth of the audience response to these very gifted young people makes me feel that the Liberace Foundation is spreading the spirit of Christmas throughout the year.

Below: A very special Christmas greeting from me to all my friends.

THE month of Christmas ends with New Year's Eve, which I usually spend at my restaurant. We hire a photographer, and I go from table to table, while he takes pictures of the guests and me. The photographs are delivered (free of charge, of course) to their tables before their dinners are over. It's the one souvenir I'm delighted to have my guests take away with them.

One year, I did an impromptu show for all the dinner guests in the ballroom. During my costume change, the band played on, and we served champagne. It was such a huge success that people expect me to do it every year. The trouble is—I don't know if I can afford me!

My All-Time Favorites

WHAT an exciting world awaits those gifted young people who've won the Liberace scholarships, if they can roll with the punches. It all depends on how they handle fame in show business—and it's all show business, whether it's pop or classical music. Nobody can tell me Vladimir Horowitz or Pavarotti is any less a showman than Bruce Springsteen or Sinatra. Celebrity is wonderful if you think of it as the icing, but it can't hide any bad ingredients underneath it. If I wanted the whole cake, I learned I had to work at it and give it my all. The audience deserved no less. I never forgot they were paying me and not the other way around.

From the time I met Paderewski when I was a boy, I've always been totally in awe of the great talents and legendary performers. I used to say, at the beginning of my career, if I ever met Toscanini, I'd faint. Well, I did meet him, and I was very proud of myself, because I didn't faint. We shook hands. He was very pleasant, very accessible—that is one of the secrets. The ones who are not accessible spend too much energy, which should go into their work, fighting with the press, punching photographers, breaking cameras, when they actually should be grateful that anybody's interested in taking their picture.

My admiration for people in my profession is governed not only by their talent but by their ability to handle success. Many performers become has-beens before their time. Those who endure seem to mature both physically and artistically. There's a lot more to fame

> The best thing about the holidays is hearing from all my good friends.

than money and worldly goods, and many performers burn themselves out much too soon. Just look at the celebrity billboards on Sunset Boulevard in Hollywood. They are ever-changing, and many
"names" never appear more than once. One begins to wonder,
"Whatever happened to so-and-so?"

I've read many biographies of the legendary artists and am always
surprised to learn they've endured many disappointments, many crit-
icisms and, great as they were, their share of flops. These people were
subject to the same human frailties as you and I. I keep that in mind
when something happens that's devastating or terribly embarrassing.
I tell myself I'm too close to this problem, but how many people in the
audience are going to know or care? It's part of life. Take it with a
grain of salt and move on.

An audience can spot a phony. Whether it's a classical, pop, or rock
concert, people love sincerity and integrity. There have been performers who've been disappointing to me because I felt they were just
going to take the money and run. And then there are others—like
Jennifer Holliday, who almost literally sings her guts out. How can
you not be moved by the intensity of feeling you get from that kind of
performer? There aren't many around capable of giving an audience
that charge. Judy Garland was one, Elvis Presley another.

I remember going to see Elvis in 1969, in Las Vegas, when he made
his so-called comeback. He was thrilling; he was electric. When I
went to see him again a few years later, he was just going through the
motions. I sat there and cried, because I knew how great he'd been
capable of being, and how he just sort of threw it away.

I was at the white heat of my television fame, and playing in Vegas,
when Elvis came to town for his first engagement. He booked in with
Freddy Martin's orchestra, an odd combination of entertainment, a
bad booking for the youngster. Musically, they were a million miles
apart. Elvis was a teenage sensation, but the people in Vegas didn't
know what to make of him. He lacked the showmanship, production,
costumes. He opened the show and then was supposed to introduce
Martin but, on opening night, he was so nervous he couldn't even
remember Freddy's name.

Elvis's manager, Colonel Parker, came to see me. He said, "My
boy"—as he used to call him—"is appearing across the street. He's
havin' some problems . . ."

He told me what was happening and then added, "He admires you
so much. If I could bring him over for a picture, he'd really appreciate
it."

Elvis came. We switched jackets. I held his guitar, while he sat at
the piano. That photograph went all over the world. One thing about
Elvis. He never forgot a friend. Every opening night, I got a guitar

Left: Swapping instruments and jackets
with the very young Elvis Presley.

made of fresh flowers. At first, I thought it was Colonel Parker who was sending them but, when I later ran into Elvis, he asked if I got his flowers. He added, "I only send them to people I love, you know."

I was very flattered that he considered me a friend, but I've more or less come to the conclusion that it's a lot easier to become famous than to remain famous. A lot of great artists, like Elvis, make a few mistakes they can't seem to overcome. It's alcohol, or drugs, or scrapes with the law, or plain bad behavior in public. They can't survive it and gradually lose their popularity.

I don't think you can take anything for granted as an entertainer. You can't wake up in the morning and think you're going to be successful for the rest of your life, so it doesn't matter what you do. Nobody can make that statement. You have to work at it, be surprising, find new things to make that audience sit up and take notice. In the final analysis, you're only as good as your last show or the one you're doing this very minute.

An audience wants only one thing. To be entertained. I don't think they're interested in anything else no matter how important it may be to the performer. As I've said, I say my prayers before going on stage, but I leave my religion in the wings. It's just too personal for that kind of exploitation. The born-agains, the former alcoholics and dopesters, who get out on a Las Vegas stage to proclaim they've found God and are now perfect, embarrass me. I wouldn't be surprised if they embarrass God, too. A casino isn't the place for that kind of confessional. If it's really true, I think their behavior, their attitude, their way with the public, should make it so obvious they don't have to say anything.

I'VE always been blessed with very loyal fans. Some of my earliest supporters were teenagers at the time. Now, they're parents with teenagers of their own, and they bring them to my shows. It's a very healthy situation, because I seem to grow into new generations. My audiences today consist of a wide variety of age groups. When I was playing at Radio City, they took a poll of the audience and found the majority was coming to see me for the first time. These newcomers to my performances make me feel as if we're discovering each other, yet there still seems to be that element of surprise and curiosity for those who've seen me before. When a performer's style becomes "old hat," he's soon forgotten. Fortunately, I've been able to avoid this by constantly coming up with new ideas and the unexpected.

It's true that most of my material comes from standard pop and the classics, but I always try to keep up with what's new in the music business. When the Beatles first came to America, one of their stops was the Las Vegas Convention Center, and I went to see them. They had a line of policemen in front of the stage to keep the kids back. The screams from the audience were so deafening, I couldn't hear the performers.

When I did meet the Beatles and really got to listen to them, I'm afraid they didn't impress me as performers, but I thought their music was wonderful and would live for a very long time. Although Lennon and McCartney were not great musicians, they were terrific composers.

I once did a television program with the London Philharmonic in which we played only Beatles songs. "Yesterday," "Michelle," and all those marvelous numbers stood the test of symphonic interpretation by one of the greatest orchestras in the world. After the show, people came up to me and said they never before realized how beautiful this music was.

Below: It's never too soon to make a new fan.

ONE of the perks of making it in show business is the fantastic people you meet: legendary performers, royalty, statesmen, religious leaders. I'm still surprised by the encounters with celebrities. I had the feeling they didn't consider me one of them, thought I was just a passing novelty, a flash in the pan. It gradually dawned on me this wasn't true when I noticed they wanted to remember our meetings by having a picture taken with me as much as I wanted to remember by a picture with them.

I feel lucky and humbled when I think of how my life has been enriched by these encounters. Some of them have been funny, some moving, and all unforgettable. When I was in Rome years ago, Pope Pius XII gave a private audience to my mother, some of my close associates, and me. It was one of the most thrilling moments in all of our lives, but especially for Mom. I was so grateful that my career had given me the chance to share it with her.

I've also had the honor of meeting three of our greatest presidents: Dwight D. Eisenhower, Harry S. Truman, and Ronald Reagan. I've already told about my last encounter with President Reagan. Now, let me tell you about my first meeting with "Dutch" Reagan, more than thirty years earlier. He was a president then, too—President of the Screen Actors Guild. It happened during one of my first Las Vegas engagements. He was doing a cowboy singing act with a couple of girls at the Last Frontier Hotel. We got together for some publicity shots. If anybody had foretold what the future held, he'd have been laughed out of town. The next time we met, he was Governor of California. By then, it was pretty clear Reagan was more than just another singing cowboy.

A meeting *I didn't* have with President Reagan led to a photograph I treasure. When it was announced that I was going to play my first engagement at the Kennedy Center, in Washington, D.C., I got an invitation to the White House from President and Mrs. Reagan. Unfortunately, just before I opened, the President went into the hospital to have a cancerous growth removed and, naturally, the invitation was cancelled.

My Washington hotel had made a chocolate piano filled with truffles as a welcoming gift. I thought it would be a wonderful gift for the President when he got home from the hospital. I knew I'd be gone, but I asked the hotel if they could keep it fresh and send it over to the White House with my card. The piano was sitting on the coffee table with the sun streaming in through the window. Before the staff could pick it up, the lid began to melt.

The White House had already been alerted to expect it. Because of security, sending over an edible gift was no small thing to arrange. I got a little panicky. They were expecting it, but how could I send the President a piano with a melted lid? The hotel assured me it could be repaired. I was very skeptical until I received a lovely picture of the President and Nancy with the piano. It was one of the first photographs taken of him after he got out of the hospital.

Opposite: President and Mrs. Reagan with the chocolate piano.
Below: Ron and Nancy Davis Reagan during their movie star days. Ron and I were both doing shows in Las Vegas.

HE very first time I was invited to play at the White House was for President Truman. I was so thrilled that I brought along gifts of small ceramic pianos and my latest record albums for the President and for Margaret. I had these two packages under my arm when I joined the reception line. This big Secret Service man came up to me and asked what was in the packages. I replied, "Just a couple of presents for the President and his daughter."

He said he'd take charge of them. I protested that I wanted to give them personally. He took the packages away, assuring me he'd see to it that the President got them.

I looked at him suspiciously. I'd read enough spy stories to know you couldn't trust the Secret Service. When the President reached me and was shaking hands, I leaned over and whispered, "I brought you a couple of presents. Make sure you get them."

*A*S with most entertainers, my favorite recollections are the "pro stories," which are about the funny things that happen when one show-business professional encounters another show-business professional. Milwaukee is famous for three things: Hildegarde, beer, and me. On one of my opening nights, I heard Hildegarde was out front and made sure she was invited to the press reception after the show. I asked her to sit next to me, so I could introduce her. I said, "Ladies and gentlemen, I'd like

Below: George and I entertain for Angie on her wedding day.

you to meet a dear friend of mine of many years. She used to be one of the world's most famous chanteuses—"

At that point, Hildegarde interrupted, "What d'you mean—used to be? I still am!"

She was right. Last year, she celebrated her eightieth birthday with a concert at Carnegie Hall. And she's still going strong!

Above: The Last of the Red Hot Mamas, Sophie Tucker and I doing our thing at one of my Hollywood parties.
Overleaf Left: Accompanying Jack Benny.
Overleaf Right: Duet for four hands. The other pair belongs to Victor Borge.

WHEN I had my house in the Hollywood Hills, one of my neighbors was the film producer Hunt Stromberg, Jr. On New Year's Eve, we were both giving parties. He called shortly before midnight and asked me to come over just to play

"Auld Lang Syne." I didn't feel I could refuse, because we were very good friends and he'd given me one of my schnauzers.

When I entered Hunt's lovely home, he came up to greet me with a strikingly beautiful woman. I thought he'd asked if I didn't think she looked like Hedy Lamarr and I said, "Hedy Lamarr should look so good."

She said, "I *am* Hedy Lamarr."

She smiled and added she'd forgive me, if I'd play for them. She took my hand and led me toward the piano. To cover my embarrassment, I babbled, "Please, forgive me. You look so great. And you've got to remember I was only a kid when I saw you in *Ecstasy*."

She moaned. "Oh, stop. Stop, already!"

After I finished playing "Auld Lang Syne," a woman asked, "Do you know any of the songs from *Annie Get Your Gun*?"

"Yeah. Who wants to know?"

"Betty Hutton." I looked right at her and asked, "Is she still around?"

"I am Betty Hutton."

I tell you—it wasn't one of my better nights. Maybe we celebrities should wear name tags like they do at conventions just so we'll recognize each other.

Below: Piano lesson from the beloved clown Emmet Kelly.

Above: It's Durante by a nose.

ONE evening, I was dining at The Four Seasons restaurant, in New York City. I saw a man at a table across the room and called over the captain to ask if it was Alfred Hitchcock. He said it was, and I wondered if it would be in bad taste to send him a little note. The captain assured me Hitchcock would love it and gave me a menu. I wrote on it, "Dear Mr. Hitchcock. I'm one of your greatest fans." I signed it and drew a little piano.

I watched out of the corner of my eye as he looked at the menu. He took a pen, quickly scribbled across it, and sent it back.

I thought, "Oh, my God, he's insulted. What'll I do now?" Under my signature he'd written "Likewise," and had drawn the famous little caricature of himself in silhouette.

A LOT of my associates used to think I owned too much real estate, but I couldn't hold a candle to Mae West. I was having lunch with the legendary lady at her Malibu beach house when a maid came in with a telephone and told her she thought it was a very important call. Miss West got on the phone and said, "Yes . . . oh, is that right? How nice . . . I appreciate it very much."

I wondered what the cryptic conversation was all about but didn't ask. I just hoped she'd tell me. She said, "What a lovely bit of news. Some years ago, I bought some land in the Valley. And I forgot all about it. They just told me they sold it for seventeen million dollars. That's seventeen million dollars I didn't know I had. Isn't that lovely news?"

I had to agree. It was lovely. Just "loverly."

I 'VE been fortunate enough to meet all kinds of off-beat and wonderful characters because of my career in show business. No matter how eccentric some of them may be off stage or screen, most of them share one characteristic in their work. It's total professionalism. My personal list of favorite performers, old and new, is marked by this quality plus a complete individuality. Others may try to copy them, but they are the originals, truly one of a kind, and different in every way from one another. See if you agree with my list, which doesn't change through the years: it just keeps growing. I like to keep an open mind about new performers, some of whom I feel will be around for a long time.

Below: Who says I always look like I've just stepped out of a band box?

The same goes for certain television actors, like Tony Danza and the cast of "Who's the Boss?" "The Golden Girls" are all superb—Bea Arthur, Betty White, Rue McClanahan, and especially Estelle Getty. I love shows like "Dynasty" and "Dallas" and "Dynasty II, the Colbys" because of superb casts and great story lines. I love soap operas, my favorites being "Days of Our Lives" and "Another World." When it comes to individuals, my preferences include a very wide range. We can start with Johnny Carson and go on from there.

SINGERS (FEMALE)

Beverly Sills, Leontyne Price, Barbra Streisand, Jennifer Holliday, Patti LaBelle, Whitney Houston, Dionne Warwick, Nell Carter, Eydie Gormé, Dolly Parton.

SINGERS (MALE)

Frank Sinatra, Pavarotti, Julio Iglesias, Michael Jackson, Bruce Springsteen, Kenny Rogers, Willie Nelson, Sam Harris, Steve Lawrence, Lionel Ritchie, Johnny Mathis, Barry Manilow. And there are singers never to be forgotten, like Elvis and Caruso. No one will ever take their place.

MOVIE ACTRESSES (FEMALE)

Bette Davis, Goldie Hawn, Meryl Streep, Jessica Lange, Angela Lansbury, Ingrid Bergman, Elizabeth Taylor, Joan Crawford, Sally Fields, Cissy Spacek, Ellen Burstyn, Cloris Leachman, Patricia Neal, Shirley MacLaine, Liza Minnelli, Anne Baxter, Anne Bancroft, Brooke Shields. Any movie with Judy Garland, Greta Garbo, or Fred Astaire and Ginger Rogers.

Opposite: Paul Weston and I don't look too happy with the take during a Columbia recording session. Below: Cary James and I backstage at THE RINK with the show's stars, Liza Minnelli and Chita Rivera.

MOVIE ACTORS (MALE)

I collect all the movies of legendary stars, like Clark Gable, Jimmy Stewart, Bogart, Spencer Tracy, Jimmy Cagney, Valentino, Robert Taylor, Cary Grant, and of more recent stars, like Chevy Chase, George C. Scott, Eddie Murphy, Billy Crystal, Michael J. Fox, John Travolta, Clint Eastwood, Burt Reynolds, Tom Selleck, Raul Julia, Ryan O'Neal. I also love some of the old-time comedians, like Laurel and Hardy, the Marx Brothers, Abbott and Costello, and I'm a great fan of Jackie Gleason and Art Carney, who are still going strong on television and in the movies.

My favorite television shows of all time are "I Love Lucy" and "The Honeymooners," and I love the return shows of "Burns and Allen." I wish they would bring back the Ed Sullivan shows. Many stars were introduced and made on that series. I also miss the comedy of Red Skelton, and who could be more individual than Jack Benny and Jimmy Durante? I had the great pleasure of guesting on all these shows when they were on television.

Thanks to home video cassettes, some of these films and television shows can be enjoyed today, and the list of recording artists, both past and present, is endless. Yes, it's true, the past can be new again when it comes to music and entertainment. Many of the extravaganza production shows in Las Vegas are really like Busby Berkeley films, in which he glamorized the stars of yesterday by surrounding them with great productions, casts that numbered in the thousands, and camera angles that were unsurpassed.

CHAPTER 11

The Best- and Worst-Dressed Awards

*T*HESE days, we seem to be less and less allowed to make up our own minds about things. Instead, they take a poll and try to convince us the result is what we should be thinking. They have polls about everything, from who's going to get elected, to what's the best television show, to who makes the best laxative. In recent years, I've found myself listed in many polls relating to the clothes I wear. In the same year, I've made the Best- and Worst-dressed lists. It can be very confusing. My stage wardrobe and my street clothes are vastly different. I never know which is being singled out for the "honor." You know, I begin to think the only certain thing about lists and polls is they're big business, and the people doing them are making a lot of money.

I'm the first to admit my stage costumes have become a very expensive joke, but I have fun with them, and the audience shares that fun with me. They'd feel cheated if I didn't wear some of these "outlandish creations." It wasn't always that way. When I first started on my television series, which had a very simple but popular format, I wore one suit. When I branched out and started to play in very large theaters, I felt a need for some pizzazz. That's how the costume thing began. It was amazing how many fellow-performers resented it. After stopping to greet one of them at a reception, I could hear the derogatory remarks as I walked away. Who's he kidding? Did you ever see such a ridiculous costume? I never let it bother me. It was as if somewhere in the back of my mind I knew someday the guy who was making the crack would be copying me.

Guess who?

Little by little, I discovered it was happening. There were some years in our business in which a performer could walk out on stage in a pair of torn or dirty jeans and a ripped shirt and get by with it. Those years are over. Now, the public demands a certain amount of escapism and fantasy from performers. The ones who dare to give it are the ones who skyrocket, like Michael Jackson and Prince. Even at rock concerts, the Madonnas and Boy Georges are the sellouts. That star-spangled shirt of Bruce Springsteen's isn't exactly your typical Army-Navy surplus. The contemporary performer is very into what used to be considered bizarre.

Below: I wonder who designed their costumes?

When I first started the fancy costumes, I guess a lot of people weren't ready for it, but I didn't let it stop me. I'd begun to discover, if I was going to be any kind of show-business leader, I had to go a few steps beyond the accepted. Through exaggeration, I could get my point across much more easily. I had to dare a little bit. Who am I kidding—I had to dare a lot. Don't wear one ring; wear five or six. People ask how I can play with all those rings, and I reply, "Very well, thank you."

It's the same in everything. When you're doing something you believe in, you've got to stick to it. It isn't always easy. It's very tempting to listen to the wrong people, who'll say, "Why do you want to gamble? You'd better not take a chance. You're not going to get away with it."

If you're true to yourself, the same people who started by being negative about what you were doing are the ones who egg you on to keep trying new tricks. I'll give you a small example. As a gag, I once bought a red-white-and-blue leather hot-pants outfit, which I thought would be fun to wear to a Halloween party. That night, I put the outfit on under a coat and came backstage for a performance, thinking it would get a laugh out of the musicians and crew. They flipped over the outfit. It wasn't expensive, it wasn't glamorous, but it was funny, extremely funny. They told me, "You've got to wear that onstage." I replied, "First, I come out in jewels and fabulous costumes, and then you want me to walk out wearing these ridiculous-looking hot pants? No way!"

They dared me to do it. I've never been one not to take a dare. I thought I couldn't just walk out. I'd have to do a number that had something to do with the patriotic colors. Ray Arnett and I put our heads together and came up with something that would get either the biggest hand or the biggest jeer of my career.

I marched down the aisle of the theater wearing the hot pants and twirling a baton like a drum major. It was a show stopper. The audience rose to a standing ovation.

Shortly after, I was booked for an Australian tour, and they wrote the hot pants into the contract. I had to wear them. When I first came onstage in Sydney, wearing one of my jeweled costumes, there was a sprinkling of flash bulbs, but the minute I appeared in the hot pants, there was a blaze. The picture made every front page in Australia and circled the earth.

Although the hot pants started as a joke, most of my costumes are not merely impromptu gags. I've done research on them. I've gone through hundreds of costume photographs, sometimes of stars like Valentino, Errol Flynn, Basil Rathbone, the swashbuckling heroes of the movies. When a costume has appealed to me, I've brought the picture to my costumer and told him how I loved it, and that he had to do something like it for me.

When he had finished embroidering the sparkle and jewels, I'd arrive for a fitting. After changing in the dressing room, I'd come out, and he was often amazed. It might have been a very intricate costume, an absolute replica of the original, with as many as eight parts. He'd say, "I didn't give you any instructions. How did you know what goes on top of what? How did you get it right?"

Below: With Hulk Hogan at Wrestlemania.

Opposite: Wearing the joke costume that was written into the contract.

I'd try to pass it off with a joke. If it was a Valentino costume, I'd explain my mother was a fan and gave me Valentino as a middle name. But it was more than that.

I haven't thought much about the afterlife, but I think I believe in former lives. I know there are certain periods of history I feel comfortable in. When I put on a costume of that period, it's almost as if I've worn it before. I just know how to arrange it. It seems natural. Sometimes, my whole manner, my attitude, changes. I relate to the person who might've been wearing it in the past.

Below: Tickled by a record store display just before my Hollywood Bowl concert.

OFFSTAGE, the things I wear very much reflect the life I live today. I try to separate the man from the performer. My street clothes are quite subdued. I always look well groomed and my best when I go out in public. I was brought up that way. When

I was a kid, I wore a lot of my older brother's hand-me-downs. They may have been patched but were always neat and clean. I wore them with pride. I can't stand the "sloppy" look, although it's quite popular with certain other performers.

My "straight," or "civilian," wardrobe has a lot of variety but none of the glitter of my costumes. What I choose to wear depends very much on where I happen to be and what I'm doing. In Malibu, I'm very casual. The people there usually wear shorts, tennis outfits, jump or leisure suits, and I dress just like my neighbors.

Although Palm Springs is also casual, it's a little more social and crowded with visitors. I'm always running into strangers who recognize me on the street or in the market, so I try to be a little more formal without being overdressed. There are also a lot of dressy social events, like benefits and openings, to which I'm invited. At these, they expect a touch of Liberace the entertainer. They want me to wear something a little bit fancier than an ordinary suit and tie. If I ever showed up in a conventional dinner jacket, they'd probably think I rented it, that Liberace couldn't possibly own anything that ordinary (although, believe me, I do). For example, I wore a white tuxedo to the Sinatra party for President Reagan, with a beautiful diamond pin on my tie. I also wore some of my rings and a full-length coat. I never wear any part of my stage wardrobe to a social event.

Opposite: Sightseeing in London in my white Rolls circa 1969.
Below: My personal wardrobe with nary a rhinestone in sight.

I HAVE a special wardrobe for traveling. When most people travel, they look kind of rumpled and comfortably disheveled. I can't afford that luxury because, when I'm traveling, I have to become Liberace again. I never know what's going to meet me at the other end of the line. Sometimes there's a press conference or, at the very least, a group of photographers and airport reporters.

The first paragraph of any story about me is usually a description of what I'm wearing. I learned years ago the press actually expected me to dress the same way I did on stage. It's something I've never done and refuse to do. They used to ask if I'd brought a change for the photographs, a gold jacket or something. My standard reply was, "What you see is what you get. If you want the glitz, you've got to pay to see it in the theater." Nevertheless, I do know the press has a job to do, and I'm a part of it, so I've devised this travel wardrobe. I wear a fur jacket, something elegantly informal. I have some outstanding sports jackets—not costumes, but expressly made to be a little showy and photogenic.

*M*EN'S fashions are really an interesting subject for analysis. Garments that go out of style usually return in ten or twenty years and are "in" again. I've learned to almost never discard my old clothes, because they always seem to come back into fashion. It's certainly true of those oversized suits and coats (very "in" now) that I wore twenty years ago. What the English call "bags," pleated trousers with a baggy look, are back again. Then there's always the constant change of the shapes of ties— wide, narrow, or no tie at all, like Don Johnson in "Miami Vice." I can remember when T-shirts were considered a part of men's underwear, and now they're seen even under tuxedos. Those with printed logos and clever sayings have become a big business, especially at rock concerts.

At the more expensive end of men's clothes, I resent a designer's name sewn on the outside of garments as a status symbol or for snob appeal. I always remove it if it's visible and let the quality and fit of the clothes speak for themselves. As far as I'm concerned, the only GG I'm interested in is Greta Garbo, and the thought of Calvin Klein's name branded on my backside is not a very appealing one. They say clothes make the man, but lately people act as if clothes make the designer. Along similar lines, I also don't approve of the blatant name letters on expensive sports cars like the Porsche. Just give me a discreet RR on the hood: that's elegance enough.

Below: Bob Hope and I backstage at the Merv Griffin Show.

The Collector

I GUESS I am what is called an incurable collector. I can be at the most prestigious antiques shop on Madison Avenue one day and at a garage sale the next and get the same kind of charge out of a find in both places. For the garage sales, I take Dorothy along, because she's so much better at bargaining, as well as having the capacity for sharing the fun of it. We've found treasures like the kitchen lamp I redid, out-of-print books, and old records that were issued years ago and are no longer available.

In the antiques shops, I have the "eye" I seem to be lucky enough to have been born with. Somehow, I can see beyond the dirt, and peeling paint, and tarnish, and spot a thing of value underneath. I've brought things home that have astonished friends. They'd ask what on earth I was doing with that piece of junk and advise me to get rid of it. The next time they'd see it was after it was restored, and the question would be where I'd found an objet d'art so beautiful. "Remember that piece of junk you told me to get rid of? This is it."

The only thing a collector regrets is the treasures he's missed buying. Occasionally, my financial advisers have worried about the amount of money I was spending on my "habit." The things I've bought have given me great pleasure, and most of them have increased in value. I spend a lot of time in Las Vegas. If you want to talk money, think how much worse it would be if I was an incurable gambler instead of an incurable collector.

Right: There's nobody home but me. All those cars are mine.

When I first began to make big money, I had no knowledge about antiques and wasn't even interested in them. I had a house in Sherman Oaks, the one with the famous piano-shaped pool, which was very push-button, very modern. I thought that was the way to go— with the latest gadget, the last word in this, that, and the other thing. It was the early fifties and where I was at in those days. My taste was very sleek, up to the minute, and, I guess, "safe."

Hollywood was no place to look for anything with age. Barely a half century before, the whole town was nothing but an orange grove. The antiques bug bit during a European tour in the mid-fifties. Suddenly, I was surrounded by these buildings and objects of incredible age. It was the historical part that really got to me. Everything had a story that went back for centuries. I'd always been interested in history. Maybe, the first time I put a candelabrum on a piano, it wasn't only an attention-getting prop but a subconscious expression of that feeling for the past I was becoming so aware of on the trip.

It was long before collecting antiques became fashionable. Europe was just recovering from the war, and money was scarce. People were

Below: The famous piano pool in my first Los Angeles home.

selling heirlooms that had been in their families for generations for anything they could get for them. You didn't have to be very knowledgeable to make the most wonderful buys. For a new collector, it was like being a child let loose in a candy store.

As late as the sixties, it was still possible to find bargains in out-of-the-way places. I was playing in Liverpool, England, and, while sightseeing, came upon a warehouse with boarded-up windows. It was owned by a Mrs. Maitland, who bought up the entire contents of great estates their owners could no longer afford to keep. Her stock was piled high to the ceilings. By then, I'd begun reading everything I could get my hands on about antiques and was learning how to tell the authentic from the fake. By looking at the hallmark stamped on the bottom of a piece of silver, I knew when it was made and by whom. When you really discover what the hallmarks mean, it's like reading history. Educating my eye was like developing a special new talent I didn't know I had.

At Mrs. Maitland's, I found many treasures, most of which were sterling silver. As I paid only a pound or ten shillings for each of them, I could send them home as "unsolicited" gifts under ten dollars.

One of the dancers in my show turned out to have quite an eye of his own. He bought a painting from Mrs. Maitland for forty pounds (one hundred dollars back then). It was later authenticated as a genuine Sir Godfrey Kneller, a portrait painter born in the seventeenth century who has a monument dedicated to him in Westminster Abbey. It's probably worth a thousand times what he paid for it.

Below: Part of my crystal collection.

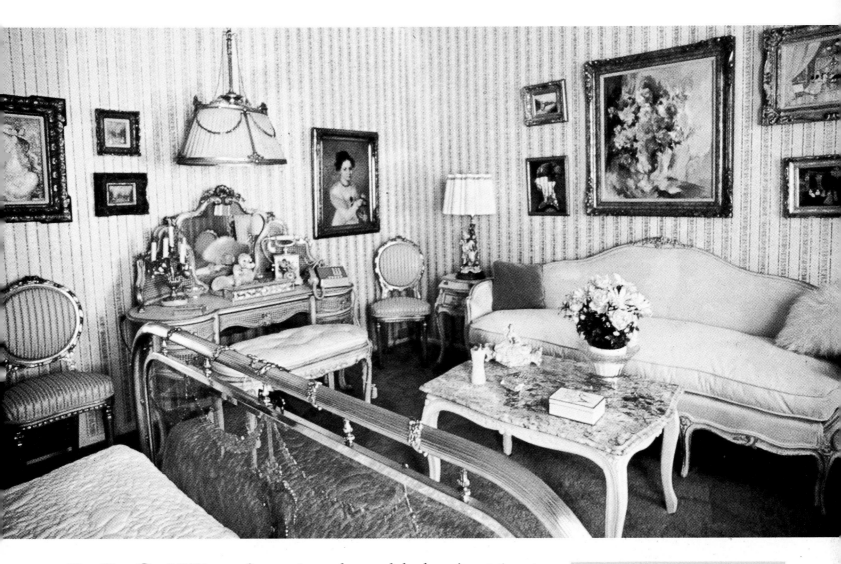

WHEN a performer is on the road, he hasn't got time to do much more than walk around and window-shop. That's so much more fun and rewarding when you have a purpose instead of just wandering aimlessly in some strange town. When I first started getting serious about collecting, I'd tear out the antiques-shop lists from the yellow pages. It wasn't my fingers that did the walking; I did, as I tried to get to all of them. My motto was—look for the white elephant. There's usually somebody who thinks he has a white elephant that turns into a treasure with a little work, and the price is always right.

In Pensacola, Florida, I bought out an entire private museum collection. Its owner, an elderly lady, was tired of possessions. She just wanted to take an extended world cruise in return for all her material goods. The price of the ticket for that cruise was twelve thousand dollars. In exchange, I wound up with three, huge moving vans of antique furniture and crystal chandeliers. Among the pieces was a fabulous Louis XV desk that had belonged to Tsar Nicholas II. Talk about history, it was on this desk that Nicholas's father, Alexander III, signed the Franco-Russian Alliance on New Year's Eve, 1893. In a way, the father sealed on the desk the son's doom. That treaty led to

the two countries entering World War I as allies, which brought on the Russian Revolution and the assassination of Nicholas II, his wife, and children.

This desk backed up a feeling I was beginning to have about my antiques. In my mind, they have a voice that can tell me all kinds of fascinating things. I let my imagination run a little wild when I'm around an object I've studied. Just think, I say to myself, this was present when such and such happened, and these historical personages were there. Occasionally, I get a little bit carried away. On an interview I once mentioned I collect Napoleonic pieces and that, when I'm in a room with them, I sometimes feel like Napoleon.

A well-known woman painter heard the program and painted me as Napoleon, complete with tricorn hat. When I first saw the picture, I thought, if I could look like that, I wouldn't be at all unhappy, and I hung it in the room with my Napoleonic collection.

Opposite: The fireplace in the
Moroccan room.
Above: My shell collection proves I am
just a beachcomber at heart.
Overleaf: Working at the priceless Czar
Nicholas desk.

*T*HE collecting was getting a little out of hand. It was beginning to move me out of my house, and I had to get a warehouse. One solution to my overstock was to open an antiques shop. It turned out not to be the best idea. A collector and dealer are two opposite things. A collector wants to keep, and a dealer wants to get rid of merchandise. I kept putting "sold" signs on all my favorite pieces so nobody else could buy them. That's no way to run an antiques business.

I don't know if the collecting led to expanding my real estate interests or expanding my real estate interests led to more collecting. All I know is they worked very well together. When I bought my mansion in the Hollywood Hills and The Cloister in Palm Springs, I could do my decorating around the pieces I knew I already had in the warehouse, instead of going out to buy new things. It gave me a lot of satisfaction, because the best thing to do with antiques is to live with them.

There are now three warehouses filled with everything from furniture to china (all bargains, of course), and there's got to be a limit to the number of homes I can buy to fill with them—or does there? There seems always to be "another" home that appeals to me, like the one I have my eye on in Scottsdale, Arizona, or the duplex penthouse in New York, or the "castle" I found in London, a real "bargain" that is up for grabs due to unpaid taxes.

Below: Not all my cars are Rolls Royces, but if you notice they do all have candelabra.

About the New Museum

I'VE noticed a lot of my fellow-entertainers spend a lot of time dumping problems and pain on their public, but I've always wanted mine to be part of the fun and good times. I'd like to share the public and private worlds of Liberace with my loyal and warm fans. Writing this book is part of it, but the new museum is where it will all really come together: the career, the Foundation, the collecting, the cooking, the clothes, the many things that reflect my way of life.

I first had the idea of a kind of museum years ago, when manufacturers and the public started to send me all kinds of piano-shaped gifts. I got the idea for a family-oriented amusement park, with everything in the form of a piano, which would be sort of Disneylandish.

An architect did some drawings, and I showed them on the old Mike Douglas television show. Mike asked when I'd start building, and I replied, "As soon as I can raise three million dollars."

The Douglas show was done live in those days and, when I got back to my hotel, there was a call from one of the bosses of a very powerful union. They had seen the show and didn't think three million dollars was enough. "You need at least five million dollars. And we'd like to give you the money."

I got very excited and called my business manager. He knew a lot of show-business people who'd lost money in projects with the union and had become indebted to it forever. He said, "If you team up with

Rehearsing for one of my television spectaculars.

that bunch, they'll be your bosses for the rest of your life. If a daughter gets married or a son has a confirmation, you play the gigs. Or else."

So I abandoned the project. My next attempt at a museum was in my home in Hollywood. I made an appearance on Cher's television show, and we did a very funny skit in which she played a guest at the museum. Cher was extremely popular and, during the next month, we had seventeen thousand visitors at the house. Naturally, the neighbors objected to the heavy traffic. Because of zoning, I was forced to close my home as a museum.

The idea of a museum wouldn't go away. I have so many possessions, awards, costumes, mementos. People were forever asking if they could see them, and taking crowds to warehouses wasn't a very practical idea. Opening a museum in Las Vegas seemed like the best solution. There are very few museums that honor somebody who is still living, and I was conscious of the fact that some people would think it was only an ego trip. It was then that we got the idea of setting up a foundation to give scholarships to worthy students, which are mostly supported by the tax-deductible admissions. Building the museum and setting up the exhibitions were a tremendous expense, but the idea of helping young musicians made it all worthwhile.

My brother George and his wife were the first curators and administrators. In 1980 we opened the doors, with all of thirty-eight dollars in petty cash in the till. The museum was an instantaneous success. It was something different for Vegas—a place with no gambling, a family entertainment, where folks could take their children. We got the museum on the bus tours and, within one year, were able to grant our first scholarships, to seven universities.

Below: The first Liberace Museum. Opposite: Cher and I dressed for a relaxing afternoon by the pool.

Above: With Cyndi Lauper.
Opposite: The biggest rhinestone in the world. They broke the mold after casting it.

Whenever we get an inquiry about selling to the museum an article that should be in it, we send a letter saying the museum doesn't buy pieces but receives them as donations for which a tax deduction can be taken. We've been blessed with many gifts of historical interest, such as George Gershwin's piano. We also have a piano that was used by Frédéric Chopin.

I often take friends like Dolly Parton on personally conducted tours of the museum. There's always a question about how the Gershwin piano sounds. If I sit down to play something by Gershwin, we feel awed by the fact that the number was actually composed on this instrument.

I'd never play anything but a piece by Chopin on the Chopin piano. It'd be sacrilegious to play something like "Beer Barrel Polka" on it. I have a great respect for all pianos, particularly those with a history. Although pianos look like the pachyderms of musical instruments, they're actually more delicate than violins. They have parts that deteriorate and don't last and have to be constantly restored. When I come upon an old piano, whether or not it's in a condition to be played, I wish it could talk, tell me who played on it, and where, and under what circumstances. As you can see, I'm very romantic about my favorite instrument.

THE seventeen vintage automobiles that I've used in my shows are big favorites with the crowds at the museum, but one of the most unique attractions is the largest rhinestone in the world. It was made especially for me by the Austrian makers of all the rhinestones I use on my costumes and props. The head of the company jokingly says I keep them in business. If you consider the size of my orders, it may not be such a joke.

They will never again create a stone as large as the one in the museum. They broke the mold. It took many attempts to make one this size and months to get it perfect. They used the finest diamond cutters to fashion its countless facets. The workmanship and size make it much more valuable than many real diamonds. To give you an example, it cost several thousand dollars for Elizabeth Taylor to have a glass copy made of one of the diamonds given to her by Richard Burton. As impressive as that diamond is, it's only a tiny fraction of the size of my rhinestone, so you can just imagine how much it is worth.

*B*ETWEEN donations from outside sources and my own collecting, we've gotten so many new acquisitions that the museum is beginning to bulge at the seams. The time has come to build again, which, as you may guess, is not exactly an idea that daunts Liberace. The new museum will be at least four times the size of the present one. Going back to the original idea of a piano-oriented park, it'll be in the shape of a piano, the largest building in that form anywhere in the world. The added space is going to allow me to do all kinds of things I just don't have room for in the present building. For example, I have about two hundred costumes hanging in cases behind sliding glass doors. These garments weren't made to be seen on hangers. There is no way of fully appreciating the elaborate workmanship when they're displayed in that manner. I've got a much more exciting idea for them.

A mannequin service is going to make a series of mannequins that resemble me. I'm trying to get away from the roped-off look of most museums. The mannequins are going to be dressed in the costumes and displayed with appropriate props and interesting lighting that will make them look the way they did when I wore them in live performances.

Below: With two of my favorite objects, a piano and a car.
Overleaf: One of the displays in the Liberace Museum.

I'm going to have a movie theater seating about three hundred people, similar to the one at the MGM Grand in Las Vegas, where the audience sits in comfortable lounge chairs and is brought refreshments while watching all the old MGM classic films. Videos of my own television series, as well as of my guest appearances on all the other great shows of the golden age of television, will be shown for an additional admission fee, which will be contributed to the Foundation. These videos will be seen by a new generation, which was too young for the originals. I'm sure their enthusiasm will give a new life to this great entertainment of the past. You just have to think of what's happening with the re-releases of "The Honeymooners" and "Burns and Allen" to know what I mean. They're getting higher ratings than most of the new shows.

The plans also call for a small outdoor amphitheater. I may appear there occasionally, but the real object will be to present concerts by some of my protégés and the scholarship winners. Again, the proceeds will go to the Foundation.

An award-winning architect and I got together to discuss the plans for the new museum. I guess I've never been one to think small, and the more we talked, the larger the idea got. Instead of just a museum, it is going to be a complex set in an exquisitely landscaped park, com-

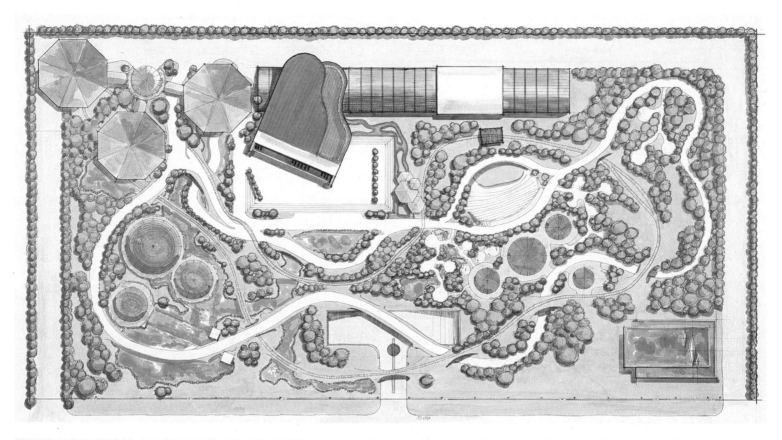

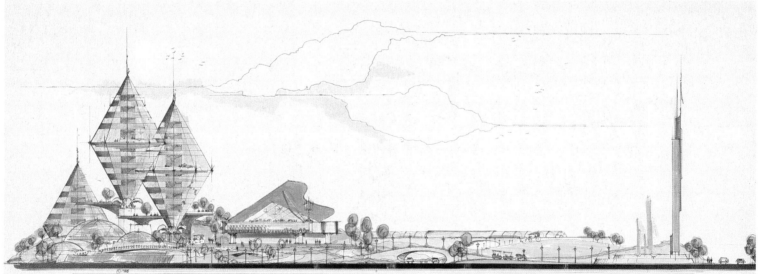

Above: Plans for the new Liberace
Museum and Park.

plete with reflection pools and fountains that keep time to music—
"The Dancing Waters" with which I've been associated. There'll be
no automobiles in the park, except the antique cars in the museum.
The parking area will be screened off by artificially created hills, and
shuttle buses will bring people from it to the complex. At one point,
the architect got a little carried away and sketched in a miniature rail-
road. I said, "This isn't Disneyland. It's Liberace Park. No railroads."

The park will also have several elegant shops (Rodeo Drive, eat
your heart out) in a beautiful mall. They'll sell all of the things with
which I'm associated, from fabulous fur creations by my furrier, to
custom-designed jewelry, to crystal creations from the rhinestone
factory in Austria. There will be outlets for all of the products we're
beginning to license under the Liberace name: like designer clothes,
cosmetics, and fragrances. There's even going to be a bank. Several
banking firms are vying for it because of the ideal location. Why not a
Liberace Bank? For years, I've been telling my audiences that I cry all
the way to the bank. Now, I'll own it.

An office-condominium complex, privately owned and overlook-
ing the park, will be built of glass and steel in the shape of (what else?)
diamonds.

The park will be built on land adjacent to my Tivoli Gardens Restaurant. I already own five acres, and, if that's not enough, I've an
option on another five. For those who don't want to have a full meal at
the restaurant, the park will be studded with a series of attractive
gazebos serving desserts, special pizzas, and other ethnic snacks. The
one thing they *won't* be is your typical fast-food operation. They'll be
managed by my people from the Tivoli Gardens, with the same high
standards of elegance and service. Beauty and elegance will be the
keynotes of the entire complex. If I didn't think we could achieve that,
I wouldn't even embark on such a mammoth undertaking. Why, even
the airlines are planning to reroute their approaches to the airport so
they can point out Liberace Park as one of the highlights of Las Vegas.

***

*L*IKE all my most wonderful dreams, the park was an idea
with the built-in nightmare of finding the finances to make
it come true. When I first discussed it with my friend
Donald Trump, he gave me some great advice. Donald is the young
real estate wizard who's changed the skyline of New York City. When
starting a project like this, you have to decide what is most important,
make that your top priority, and go from there. He said, "The trouble

with you is you think you have to earn this money before you start. It'll never happen that way. You never use your own money."

That was news to me, and I wondered what he meant by it. He explained there were people with only one talent, and that was for making money. They had money to burn. They were looking for ways to spend it to make money. To do that, they went after people like a Donald Trump, or a Walt Disney, or, why not, a Liberace—people who were creative enough to envision the fantasies in which they could invest.

Donald was talking about billionaires and not mere millionaires. From his point of view, anybody could make a million. A rock star with only one platinum record was an instant millionaire. There were these people who started making cinnamon rolls for neighbors and opened a small shop. These rolls were so special people began lining up at five in the morning to buy them. They started to expand. The first year they made a profit of seven hundred fifty thousand dollars, and now they're in the three- or four-billion dollar bracket.

I guess what it came down to was that to make a million, all you had to do was build a better mousetrap. To make a billion, you had to finance a million better mousetraps invented by other people. The philosophy of using other people's money was very heady stuff for a boy who was brought up to believe debt was a dirty four-letter word. Fortunately, I didn't have to look for any billionaires, just as I didn't have to indenture myself to any union bosses.

I described the plan for office condos to Donald, and he said, "You will be okay. That's your financial starting force."

Again, I didn't understand what he meant, and he explained, "That should bring in about fifty million dollars before you ever turn a shovel in the ground. Just the concept of it. Businesses will want that space and pay for it in advance."

According to Donald Trump, I was suddenly a tycoon without even being sure what that meant. You might say this was a case of virtue being its own reward and paying dividends at the same time, for the whole enormous enterprise started with the simple and worthwhile idea of giving pleasure to a public that had been very good to me, while also helping worthy but needy students.

Before this book is published, I hope I'll have a ground-breaking ceremony for the park. I already have the silver shovel from Tiffany's for the occasion. I'm going to have it gold-plated and displayed in a glass case in the foyer for the new museum.

Walt Disney had a dream when he envisioned Disneyland, which he never got to see in its fulfillment, since he died before its completion. I'd like to experience a little of heaven here on earth (while I'm still able to) before the time comes for me to discover the "real" thing.

Opposite: My Valentine Special aboard
the Queen Mary.
Below: With Walt Disney.

Back to the Future

I STARTED this book because I'd decided to take the time to smell the roses, to enjoy and reflect on all the things that have enriched my private life. Now, it's time to get on with it, to get back to the future. It's really more natural to me, because I've never been one to live in the past. Of course it's sometimes fun to reminisce about old-time events, but they're only pleasant memories that tend to fade.

For me, every new happening far outshines the old. The future holds so many new challenges that require total energy and concentration. The best thing about the past is it helps you plan for the future by teaching you how to avoid the old pitfalls and mistakes in your attempts to surpass former triumphs.

Getting better rather than older is my driving force. This can be accomplished only by conserving the energy necessary to strive for total perfection. I used to have a tendency to spread myself too thin by accepting certain engagements that drained my energy and creativity, that were merely time-consuming and did nothing to enhance my career or give greater pleasure to my audiences. There was a time when I did so many dates I couldn't remember where I was performing from one week to the next. It was a real "it's Thursday, this must be Brussels" life. After a while, the so-called glamour and excitement were replaced by monotony and repetition, which, in a way, cheated the people who paid good money to see me and to whom I owed nothing less than my very best.

In the garden of the Coq Hardi restaurant, near Paris.

Below: Guest-starring with Phil Harris on the Andy Williams Show.
Opposite: Wrinkles and I arrange the flowers in Malibu.
Overleaf Left: Dorothy Malone and I in the final scene of "Sincerely Yours."
Overleaf Right: On the set with director Gordon Douglas.

I still find life is filled with limitless possibilities, although there are a few things I know I'll probably never try, like a "legitimate" show. I've never been able to understand how a Broadway performer can do the same show night after night, week after week, and sometimes year after year, without going stale. Yet, many of them do just that, never losing the spontaneity and excitement required by each performance. The late Yul Brynner in *The King and I* was a good example. His final performances were every bit as vital as the more than four thousand that preceded them.

With me, the minute a number becomes stale, I replace it with something new. Later on, I might put the number back in with a new twist that makes it fresh again. Sometimes, even a new costume gives an old number a new life.

Having more leisure time now gives me much greater opportunity to develop new material and to polish the old to a new brilliance. It also affords the time to concentrate on other avenues of my profession that, until now, I've had to put aside—things like writing, television appearances on dramatic shows, videos, and movies.

Ever since I did *Sincerely Yours* back in the fifties, respected filmmakers have flatteringly thought I could have a career as an actor in nonmusicals. I did my film for Warner Brothers. At the time, the great director George Stevens was on the same lot, doing his blockbuster *Giant*, with Elizabeth Taylor and Rock Hudson. Stevens would go to see my rushes every day. When we finally met, he said, "You're a born actor. I can understand why they're featuring the piano in this picture. It's what you're famous for. But I'd love to do a movie with you in which you don't go near a piano."

I was overwhelmed and thought seriously about it, but we were entering a period of pictures with subject matter that just didn't interest me. I was so busy with concerts, night clubs, and television I didn't think of films again for another ten years.

In the early sixties, I was touring England and became friends with Tony Richardson. At the time, Richardson was married to Vanessa Redgrave and was the hottest young director in London, having made such hits as *Tom Jones*, *The Entertainer*, and *Look Back in Anger*. When he was signed to come to Hollywood to direct a film version of Evelyn Waugh's novel *The Loved One*, he offered me the leading role of Joyboy. After reading the script, I discussed the project with my people. Joyboy was one of the most unsavory characters in screen history. He was an effeminate mama's boy, ten feet off the ground at all times. A great actor could get away with playing the part, because nobody would confuse him with the role he was playing. But I wasn't known as a great actor. If I did a good job, some people might think I was making fun of all of the things people respected about me. I said,

"It's a terrific part, *but*, if I do it, I'll probably have to leave the country. Or, at least, quit show business."

Even after I turned down Joyboy, Richardson still wanted me in the picture. He had the role of an unctuous casket salesman written into the picture especially for me. I loved it. I played it very seriously, never smiling once, and adored every minute of it. It was a cameo part, and my reviews were among the best for the picture. May I add immodestly, the best in that picture was pretty good, when you consider Rod Steiger ended up playing Joyboy, and the other cameos included James Coburn, Milton Berle, and Sir John Gielgud, who's probably the greatest Shakespearean actor of our time.

I don't rule out the idea of doing another major motion picture sometime in the future, but I think it'd have to include some musical numbers. The people who come to see me expect me to play. They'd be disappointed if I did a straight acting role.

Below: The Court Jester routine from one of my Vegas shows.

I'd love to do something that didn't depend upon my playing Liberace. Television is the logical place, but they keep asking me to do guest shots as myself. When "Miami Vice" asked me to do an episode playing Liberace, I replied, "I'd like them to ask me to do 'Miami Vice' but *not* as Liberace." The problem is, a lot of producers of these shows don't think they can afford me, and ordinarily they're right. But I'll let them in on a secret. If the part's right, I'll do it for what they can afford to pay me. Instead of lowering my price, I'll simply donate the fee to my Foundation. That's what I did when Linda Dano asked me to do some guest shots on "Another World."

Above: Saville Row meets Carnaby Street in London.

Left: The Muppet Show in London. I'm
the one on the left.

*T*HE future certainly includes a deep involvement in the Foundation and the museum complex. There will also be a lot of licensing and endorsements of products related to my image as a performer. These days, practically every celebrity and big-name entertainer is involved in some phase of product endorsement, whether it be coffee or pantyhose. Remember Robert Young, and Joe Namath, Joe DiMaggio, and Laurence Olivier—and where would Charmin be without Mr. Whipple?

Just think of it: someday, some future President of the United States will be wearing a suit designed by Liberace, while the First Lady's Inaugural gown will be designed by Joan Collins.

Years ago, both male and female movie legends influenced the fashion and cosmetic industries. All over the world, you could find copies of Dietrich's eyebrows, Joan Crawford's shoulder pads and shoes, Valentino's slave bracelet, as well as his slicked-back, glossy, patent-leather hairstyle. In the not so distant past, nearly every man sported a fedora like Jimmy Cagney or George Raft. They certainly never went out in public without a tie and socks. After *It Happened One Night*, the only thing they didn't wear was their undershirts. By not wearing one in that picture, Clark Gable single-handedly bankrupted several manufacturers of the garments. When Barbara Stanwyck decided hats were a headache, a thriving millinery industry packed its feathers and veils and stole away into the night.

Yesterday, it was John Travolta's white suit, and today, it's Don Johnson's pink suit, while the punk of Madonna is losing ground to the sleek of Sade. Fashions do come and go but, luckily for me, the glitter of Liberace keeps on making people happy.

There was a time when one woman might say to another, "May I borrow your lipstick?" Now, it's not unusual for one male rocker to say to another, "May I borrow your eyeliner?" And practically no man is above borrowing his friend's skin bronzer. Male cosmetics are becoming a very popular item, but they're no new phenomenon. The ancient Egyptian men wore them just about from birth right on to the mummy stage, while eighteenth-century dandies were as heavily painted as any of their ladies fair.

But getting back to the future. What lies ahead should be determined by what we've missed in the past. The present should be spent realizing all of our unfulfilled dreams and ambitions.

My attitude is that nothing is impossible—it just takes a little longer. George Burns proved that by winning an Oscar in his eighties and celebrated his ninetieth birthday by signing a five-year contract.

Remember, most of the time it's not so much what we've done in the past but what we haven't done that we regret. Making up for lost time is the best motivation of all in planning for the future.

12·25·95

Merry Christmas!

Jan

This Book Belongs to

_____

ADDRESS

_____

_____

HOME PHONE

_____

WORK PHONE

_____

FAX

_____

REWARD IF FOUND

Alexandra Stoddard's

Book of Days

Each today, well-lived,
makes every yesterday a dream of happiness
and each tomorrow a vision of hope.
Look well, therefore, to this one day,
for it and it alone is life.

—SANSKRIT POEM

Alexandra Stoddard's

Book of Days

WILLIAM MORROW AND COMPANY, INC.

New York

ISBN:0-688-13686-9

Printed in the United States of America

First Edition

1 2 3 4 5 6 7 8 9 10

DESIGNED BY MARYSARAH QUINN & MARK GAROFALO

Illustrations by Stephen Freeburg

WELCOME

*T*his is your book of life.

*Y*our year begins on the very day you find this book and make it your own. Welcome to this journal. Many joys await you as you put these pages to their best use; think of the ways in which you can turn this into more than a record of doings. Let this journal be a companion to your days and a treasured keepsake to pass down to your grandchildren.

*T*his book has been designed so that you may write down your own Grace Notes—telling clues of your love of life. Use this diary to free your imagination.

I hope your mornings, noontimes, afternoons and evenings are rich with experiences, engagements, appointments, pleasures, contentment and joy. Be open to serendipitous occurrences. Embrace the warmth, care, and kindnesses that others show you. Let every experience expand your awareness of your surroundings and your appreciation of life.

*F*inally, remember that each day is a microcosm of your life. Your positive attitude, your ability to imbue mundane activities with soul, your new directions, inspirations, insights and quests will uplift you and be a positive influence on the people you love and care about. The connections and possibilities are boundless.

*W*elcome to your book of days.

*G*race, joy, and love *every* day of the year.

Alexandra Stoddard

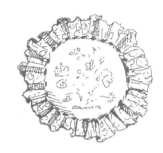

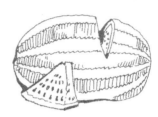

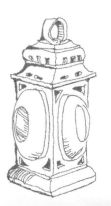

*L*ove begins at home, and it is not how much we do ... but how much love we put in that action.

—MOTHER TERESA

M AKING THE MOST
OF YOUR *BOOK OF DAYS*

J ump right in. There is no perfect day or time. Begin wherever you are and move forward. Don't be afraid to write in these beautiful pages, for without your active participation this book is meaningless. The more you use it, the more exciting your days will become. Energy and enthusiasm are infectious. Go for it.

P lace the ribbon at the start of each week, and write in the month and date at the top where indicated. If you enjoy using a fountain pen, you'll find this paper sensational. I use my usual fuchsia ink but you may change colors at whim. Experiment. You can use magic markers, colored pencils, ordinary lead pencils or ballpoint pens. It's entirely up to you. The whole point of this is to inspire you to make the most of *every day*.

M ark in the time of each appointment, meeting or event. Make notations about the weather, your mood, and what's going on around you. When you get to the end of the week, fill in "The Best Things That Happened This Week" and "Goals for Next Week." Review each day and fill the squares with notes about those special moments that occurred on the appropriate day. Record feelings, or a delicious meal you enjoyed, or a letter that gave you pleasure.

R ead the quote and Grace Note of the day and take time to reflect on the message. At the end of the week, reread them and underline the ones that resonate for you.

A s you go along, write in your own Grace Notes, the birthdays of people you love, special celebrations, the favorite things of children, lovers and friends, the gifts you plan to give, the gifts stored in your inventory, quotes, affirmations and inspirations, joys, things learned as well as a story that made you laugh. Write about your times of solitude as well as moments shared with others.

D oodle, draw, add an extra ribbon or two. Keep a cup of colored pencils close at hand to make sketches. Cross out appointments cancelled or postponed. A full book of days will be your record of a life in process: a courageous, adventurous journey.

I n these stressful and troubled times, we are all too busy to *really* live unless we purposely sit back, sip some tea and think about how we want to spend our time, who we want to share it with and then make it happen. Fill in the colorful boxes and live each moment with more zest, more fun and more pure living than ever before.

H appy days!   *Alexandra Stoddard*

NEW DIRECTIONS

It is our duty as men and women to proceed as though limits to our ability do not exist. We are collaborators in creation.

TEILHARD DE CHARDIN

Each day we're given a fresh start. Today can be the beginning of a more productive, affirming existence. Let all the pain, regrets, disappointments, and disillusions of yesterday fall from your shoulders. Don't let gray days get you down. Focus on the light. Do not dwell on problems but seek satisfying solutions.

Place a new emphasis on all the goodness in your life, all the blessings you have, your love, your children, your work, your friends, your home. Let your love of life reinforce all you do and let all your energy be used to build a better world, a place where grandchildren may be safe and find joy. Spread hope through your strength and courage and unwavering determination to live a healthy, productive, full life that rises above sorrow and defeat. Light candles, smile, sing out in praise for all you have. Take time to ritualize moments, create ceremonies and celebrations.

Vitality is self-generated. Living in this awareness gives you the energy to go the extra mile, to put your trust in everything you do. Whatever is worth doing deserves your full creative force. Never succumb to mediocrity.

Concentrate on putting some magic into every day. Stretch yourself to find out what is possible and then stretch farther: dare to do the impossible. Tap into the universal energy of love.

Alexandra Stoddard

	*S*UNDAY	*M*ONDAY	*T*UESDAY	*W*EDNESDAY
MORNING	*F*or life was freakish/And life was fervent/And I was always/Life's willing servant. STEPHEN VINCENT BENET			
NOON			*G*reat joys, like griefs, are silent. SHACKERLEY MARMION	
AFTERNOON		*W*e live by admiration, hope and love. WORDSWORTH		*O*ne of these days is none of these days. H.G. BOHN
EVENING				
GRACE NOTES	*P*articipate fully in everything you do. The more you care, the more you will accomplish. Go for it!	*M*ake a point of affirming those around you today. Begin with yourself. Offer hope and joy.	*T*here are some epiphanies that radiate and are celebrated internally.	*B*egin something new today. A poem, a journal, a family ritual. Let today be a special, memorable day.

THURSDAY	FRIDAY	SATURDAY	
	We are not hypocrites in our sleep. WILLIAM HAZLITT		*Perfect valor is to do without witnesses what one would do before all the world.* LA ROCHEFOUCAULD
		Persistent work triumphs. VIRGIL	THE BEST THINGS THAT HAPPENED THIS WEEK: ....
I am never indifferent, and never pretend to be. LONGFELLOW			GOALS FOR NEXT WEEK: ❧.......................... .... ❧.......................... ....
You can never care too much. Enthusiasm is the fire that makes you soar.	*Be direct. Acknowledge your interests and passions. Be honest with yourself and others.*	*Everything you do with love and focus will have results. Practice patient persistence.*	*Your thoughts and acts of kindness will shape your character.*

	SUNDAY	MONDAY	TUESDAY	WEDNESDAY
MORNING			One finds one's own style by finding one's own self. LIN YUTANG	
NOON	Great thoughts come from the heart. LUC DE CLAPIERS			
AFTERNOON				Anywhere is paradise. GEORGE HARRISON
EVENING		And trust me not at all or all in all. TENNYSON		
GRACE NOTES	What is your heart bursting with today? How are you going to express it?	Surround yourself with trustworthy people and don't second-guess them.	Style is not an outer trapping but an authentic understanding of your essential personality. Style polishes your essence.	Keep inside you an image of your ideal place. Whether it be a mountain, a beach or a garden, you *are* there, here.

THURSDAY	FRIDAY	SATURDAY	
		*W*hether you think you can do a thing or not, you're right. HENRY FORD	*A*nyone who keeps the ability to see beauty never grows old. KAFKA
	*T*here is always a better way. THOMAS EDISON		THE BEST THINGS THAT HAPPENED THIS WEEK: ....
I grow old ever learning many things. SOLON			GOALS FOR NEXT WEEK: ❧............................... .... ❧............................... ....
*M*y husband, Peter, has requested that his tombstone read "Still Learning." What are *you* exploring?	*N*ever settle for the mediocre. Create, invent a better way of living each day.	*F*ollow your convictions. Practice the art of the possible. Stay away from people who tell you what you can't do.	*T*oday, practice seeing everything anew and thus enrich your understanding.

	*S*UNDAY	*M*ONDAY	*T*UESDAY	*W*EDNESDAY
MORNING		*R*ipeness is all. SHAKESPEARE		
NOON			*R*eading is to the mind what exercise is to the body. SIR RICHARD STEELE	
AFTERNOON				*C*haracter is destiny. HERACLITUS
EVENING	*W*here there is no vision, the people perish. PROVERBS 29:18			
GRACE NOTES	*T*he proverb above was once chiseled on the pulpit of New York City's Heavenly Rest Church—inadvertently without the "no." Have vision!	*P*ay attention to ripeness. This applies to tomatoes, avocados, work and love.	*M*ake a list of books you want to read. What are you reading now? Are these books good for your mind? Your soul?	*C*haracter is the essential ingredient that pilots our life. Nothing is more important. Be on watch to evaluate *your* character.

THURSDAY	FRIDAY	SATURDAY	
	No man can lose what he never had. IZAAK WALTON		*We* can do anything we want to do if we stick to it long enough. HELEN KELLER
		I am not arguing with you—I am telling you. WHISTLER	THE BEST THINGS THAT HAPPENED THIS WEEK: ....
The sky is the daily bread of the eyes. EMERSON			GOALS FOR NEXT WEEK: ....
I had an art teacher who urged us to look up. The sky is our light and illumination. The sun is shining somewhere.	*Don't* focus on loss, but on what you have. Concentrate on your assets, your good qualities, your generosity of spirit.	*People* resist hearing the truth. It sometimes stings. Be yourself. There are times when telling the truth *is* necessary.	*All* my heroes and heroines are people who overcame unspeakable hardships and triumphed. They teach us to be tenacious.

	$\mathcal{S}$UNDAY	$\mathcal{M}$ONDAY	$\mathcal{T}$UESDAY	$\mathcal{W}$EDNESDAY
MORNING		$\mathcal{K}$nowledge is the food of the soul. PLATO		$\mathcal{C}$arpe diem. HORACE
NOON	$\mathcal{A}$ll intellectual improvement arises from leisure. SAMUEL JOHNSON			
AFTERNOON			$\mathcal{W}$hat if this present were the world's last night? JOHN DONNE	
EVENING				
GRACE NOTES	$\mathcal{I}$'m wisest on Sundays when I give myself time to think. A day of *businesslessness* is often a great inspirer.	$\mathcal{T}$he more we learn, the fuller our soul becomes, and yet there's always room for more.	$\mathcal{L}$ive in the consciousness of *now* being the fullness of your existence. This is no ordinary Tuesday, is it?!	$\mathcal{S}$eize the day! Seize the moment! Discover the richness of life's possibilities by expecting a lot from yourself.

THURSDAY

FRIDAY

SATURDAY

The great enemy of the truth is very often not the lie—deliberate, contrived and dishonest—but the myth—persistent, persuasive and unrealistic.
JOHN F. KENNEDY

Something will turn up.
BENJAMIN DISRAELI

THE BEST THINGS THAT HAPPENED THIS WEEK:

....
....
....
....
....
....
....

Silence is the greatest persecution. PASCAL

The greatest virtues are those which are most useful to other persons. ARISTOTLE

GOALS
FOR NEXT WEEK:

....
....
....
....
....
....
....

Go about your day doing your best, going the extra mile. Goodness enriches the life of others.

Keep studying. Read. Experiment. Einstein loved his experiments. Be a genius by trying. Seek.

Sing out in praise of those you admire, respect and love. And then be silent.

Pay attention to reality. Myths can make you miserable. There is plenty to deal with today that is real, immediate and true.

Month _____ THE WEEK OF _____ TO _____

	$\mathcal{S}$UNDAY	$\mathcal{M}$ONDAY	$\mathcal{T}$UESDAY	$\mathcal{W}$EDNESDAY
MORNING	$\mathcal{T}$ime driveth onward fast. TENNYSON			$\mathcal{W}$hat is always speaking silently is the body. NORMAN O. BROWN
NOON		$\mathcal{A}$h, but a man's reach should exceed his grasp, or what's a heaven for? ROBERT BROWNING		
AFTERNOON			$\mathcal{A}$ll the modern inconveniences. MARK TWAIN	
EVENING				
GRACE NOTES	$\mathcal{W}$e are only given a tiny slice of time. How can you hold time?	$\mathcal{S}$tretching your mind doesn't hurt. Think of what you can begin today that is beyond your grasp. Start it!	$\mathcal{D}$on't have a nervous breakdown over the so-called conveniences that don't work. Be patient!	$\mathcal{P}$ay attention to everything the body tells you. In a sense, you can become your own doctor by taking good care of yourself.

THURSDAY	FRIDAY	SATURDAY	
	*B*ut the sea never explains the flower. EDITH HAMILTON		*W*e are spinning our own fates, good or evil, and never to be undone. Every smallest stroke of virtue or of vice leaves its ever so little scar. … Nothing we ever do is, in strict scientific literalness, wiped out. WILLIAM JAMES
		*T*he present is our own. THOMAS LOVE PEACOCK	THE BEST THINGS THAT HAPPENED THIS WEEK:
			....
			....
			....
			....
			....
			....
			GOALS FOR NEXT WEEK:
I don't want to go out. I don't want out-ness. BROOKE STODDARD			➤..
			....
			....
			....
			➤..
			....
			....
*W*hy go out tonight? Stay at home, be private, cozy and surround yourself with books; play music; observe a flower.	*Y*ou will never be able to understand everything. Be yourself and be content.	*A*ll we will ever own or behold with certainty is the moment. Reflect on *now* and *live* on earth while on earth.	*B*e the architect of your fate. Think about everything as interconnecting circles. Life builds in strength, goodness and light. Start drafting.

Month _____		THE WEEK OF _____ TO _____		
	*S*UNDAY	*M*ONDAY	*T*UESDAY	*W*EDNESDAY
MORNING			*H*appiness is no laughing matter. ARCHBISHOP RICHARD WHATELEY	
NOON				*C*ome up and see me sometime. MAE WEST
AFTERNOON		*H*e begins to die that quits his desires. GEORGE HERBERT		
EVENING	*T*he feast of reason and the flow of the soul. ALEXANDER POPE			
GRACE NOTES	*W*henever we are reasonable, we are nurturing our soul. Trust common sense. Be in the flow of love.	*L*ive with expanding, grand, great desires. Plant a tree the day you die. Desire to live forever. You just may.	*H*appy people are our teachers, for they have had to overcome all their obstacles. They are spreaders of hope for all of us.	*C*all a friend today; make a date for a visit. Come see me sometime.

THURSDAY

*O*nly the educated are free.
 EPICTETUS

*N*o one, nothing can keep us from our journey. Searching, questing will assure a vital life: Education is the result.

FRIDAY

*T*o every thing there is a season, and a time to every purpose under the heaven.
ECCLESIASTES

*N*ow is the time to bring together your fresh interests with your innate talents and strengths so they may have time to be fulfilled.

SATURDAY

*W*hat I aspired to be, And was not, comforts me.
ROBERT BROWNING

*E*xpect greatness and settle for being as good as you can be, as caring as an angel.

*N*othing is little to him that feels it with great sensibility.
SAMUEL JOHNSON

THE BEST THINGS THAT
HAPPENED THIS WEEK:

....
....
....
....
....
....
....

GOALS
FOR NEXT WEEK:

....
....
....
....
....
....
....

*F*eeling everything with a sense of awe can elevate the quiet, private experience into a sacred moment.

	SUNDAY	MONDAY	TUESDAY	WEDNESDAY
MORNING			*T*here is a good within each human breast. OVID	
NOON	*R*emember when life's path is steep to keep your mind even. HORACE			
AFTERNOON				*E*very religion is good that teaches man to be good. THOMAS PAINE
EVENING		*M*ay you live all the days of your life. JONATHAN SWIFT		
GRACE NOTES	*W*hen you are experiencing your greatest hardship, choose to concentrate on your own unwavering purpose.	*M*ake today one of those magic days in whch you do an abundance of really wonderful things. What will you do?	*F*ind it. When someone is driving you crazy, light a candle and write down their virtues.	*E*mbrace each truly good human soul. Don't judge how the wisdom came into consciousness. Goodness is universal.

Month _____ THE WEEK OF _____ TO _____

$\mathcal{T}$ HURSDAY	$\mathcal{F}$ RIDAY	$\mathcal{S}$ ATURDAY	
			$\mathcal{M}$ arriage is not a goal in itself but is simply another opportunity to grow and mature. GOETHE
$\mathcal{C}$ ulture has one great passion —the passion for sweetness and light. MATTHEW ARNOLD			THE BEST THINGS THAT HAPPENED THIS WEEK: ....
		$\mathcal{D}$ o the thing and you will be given the power. EMERSON	
	$\mathcal{I}$ t is to create, and in creating live. LORD BYRON		GOALS FOR NEXT WEEK: ....
$\mathcal{T}$ here's darkness and despair in the world. Your radiance will light the way.	$\mathcal{W}$ hen you create something unique, you give birth to *your* humanity. Create something beautiful today. What?	$\mathcal{W}$ hen you know what has to be expressed, do it. Strength is always there when you're willing to dare.	$\mathcal{I}$ n my husband, Peter, I have found my other half. Our lives double in growth and possibility. Partnership is the key.

Month _____ THE WEEK OF _____ TO _____

	SUNDAY	MONDAY	TUESDAY	WEDNESDAY
MORNING				
NOON		*R*ather than love, than money, than fame, give me truth. THOREAU		
AFTERNOON	*L*ife has got to be lived—that's all there is to it. ELEANOR ROOSEVELT			*A*sk not for whom the bell tolls; it tolls for thee. JOHN DONNE
EVENING			*M*eet me by moonlight alone. JOSEPH AUGUSTINE WADE	
GRACE NOTES	*L*ife must be fully experienced. If it appears easy today, rest assured it will be difficult tomorrow. Live *all of it* for total satisfaction.	*T*ruth is a quest that helps one understand life's potential. Grace, love and light are true. Believe that truth.	*W*e're lucky if we ever meet our true love. Who have you met or will you meet by moonlight alone?	*W*hatever good you do in your corner of the world will ring bells across the universe. Let a ringing bell inspire you to act.

THURSDAY	FRIDAY	SATURDAY	
Courage is resistance to fear. MARK TWAIN			*If a man empties his purse into his head, no one can take it away from him. An investment in knowledge always pays the best interest.* BENJAMIN FRANKLIN
		The unexamined life is not worth living. SOCRATES	THE BEST THINGS THAT HAPPENED THIS WEEK: ....
	Truth must be conceived as a truth. ALBERT EINSTEIN		
			GOALS FOR NEXT WEEK: ❧................................... .... ❧................................... ....
Living is a courageous act. Dare to face challenges head on and then feel grace.	*William James believed truth is what works. Believe in what you see, the ordinary, the familiar, as long as they ring true.*	*All insight is acquired slowly. We must consciously examine our lives every day and monitor our paths.*	*Learning is a sure bet. It's exciting and it puts life's setbacks into perspective. What are you studying now?*

Month _____ THE WEEK OF _____ TO _____

	SUNDAY	MONDAY	TUESDAY	WEDNESDAY
MORNING	*Silent gratitude isn't much use to anyone.* GLADYS BERTHE STERN			
NOON		*Even a small start is worth a try.* SENATOR JOHN DANFORTH		
AFTERNOON				*Every day is a New Year.* ROSE MARIE MORSE
EVENING			*Life shrinks or expands in proportion to one's courage.* ANAÏS NIN	
GRACE NOTES	*The most appropriate time to tell someone what you think of them is at the time you extend your thanks. Praise must be expressed generously and immediately.*	*The greatest failure of all is the idea never put to use. Start today. Spare yourself the sadness of what might have been.*	*Being brave is more important than being brilliant. Brave people usually get all they need from life. Courage brings joy.*	*Embrace every dawn as an opportunity for illumination, inspiration, insight and personal growth.*

THURSDAY	FRIDAY	SATURDAY	
*F*atigue makes cowards of us all. VINCE LOMBARDI			*I* never think of the future. It comes soon enough. ALBERT EINSTEIN

THE BEST THINGS THAT
HAPPENED THIS WEEK:

....
....
....
....
....
....
....

*M*an can never escape from himself. GOETHE

*F*ind the good—and praise it. ALEX HALEY

G O A L S
FOR NEXT WEEK:

❧..
....
....
....
❧..
....
....

*W*hen our energy circuits are unplugged, we're unbrave. We feel like crawling under our sheets. Rest up so you can be courageous again.

*L*ook around you. Express gratitude to people, places and things when you find good. This is wisdom.

*Y*our attitude, your character, your every quality goes with you wherever you journey through life. Embrace, don't escape yourself.

*Y*ou and I will never wake up tomorrow. Today is what we have. The future is made of present moments. Think of *now*.

	Month _____	THE WEEK OF _____ TO _____		
	SUNDAY	**MONDAY**	**TUESDAY**	**WEDNESDAY**
MORNING	*One may measure small things by great.* VIRGIL			
NOON			*Habit is a sort of second nature.* CICERO	
AFTERNOON				
EVENING		*The mode by which the inevitable comes to pass is effort.* OLIVER WENDELL HOLMES		*I will be I!* THOREAU
GRACE NOTES	*There is no such thing as a small thing. Everything is vitally important—the sun, the shadow, the wind and your smile.*	*Whenever we move our feet we are rewarded. That's all there is to it: perseverance.*	*Look to acquire life-enhancing habits: We are, after all, what we do. Be noble in your habits. They will enrich you.*	*The faster we focus on who we are, the greater the chance of living a life of significance.*

$\mathcal{T}$HURSDAY	$\mathcal{F}$RIDAY	$\mathcal{S}$ATURDAY	
		$\mathcal{T}$here is nothing so advantageous to a man as a forgiving disposition. TERENCE	$\mathcal{O}$ne great, strong, unselfish soul in every community could actually redeem the world. ELBERT HUBBARD
	$\mathcal{I}$f you would judge, understand. SENECA		THE BEST THINGS THAT HAPPENED THIS WEEK: ....
$\mathcal{W}$hatever your advice, make it brief. HORACE			
			GOALS FOR NEXT WEEK: ❧.................................. .... ❧.................................. ....
$\mathcal{N}$o one wants to hear a long, drawn-out story of what should be done. Make your point and let go.	$\mathcal{T}$hink of yourself as a mirror. Everything you think, feel and judge could be you.	$\mathcal{F}$orgive and forget. Every day should potentially be a fresh start.	$\mathcal{R}$eflect on all the giving souls you know who make a difference. What is it about their spirit that makes them shine?

	SUNDAY	MONDAY	TUESDAY	WEDNESDAY
MORNING		*D*on't find fault, find a remedy. HENRY FORD		
NOON	*U*nto ourselves our own life is necessary; unto others, our character. ST. AUGUSTINE			
AFTERNOON				*W*e cannot go back. WITOLD RYBCZYNSKI
EVENING			*E*very noble work is, at first, impossible. THOMAS CARLYLE	
GRACE NOTES	*W*hether we like it or not, our actions reveal our character. Good deeds speak of integrity. Be decent and life will be beautiful.	*E*veryone is quick to point out problems. What's noble is to find solutions. This is an ongoing challenge. What are your solutions for today?	*E*verything appears too difficult until we commit ourselves. Don't dream scared. Dream of the impossible and work miracles into your life.	*S*ift through the sands of your past to find the gold. Look at it, don't carry it; travel light.

It is no use saying "We are doing our best." You have got to succeed in doing what is necessary.

WINSTON CHURCHILL

Ask, and it shall be given you; seek, and ye shall find; knock, and it shall be opened unto you.   MATTHEW 7:7

THE BEST THINGS THAT HAPPENED THIS WEEK:

....
....
....
....
....
....
....

Happiness and beauty are by-products.

GEORGE BERNARD SHAW

While we teach, we learn.

SENECA

GOALS
FOR NEXT WEEK:

....
....
....
....
....
....
....

An artist friend wrote books to learn about a subject. We gain inspiration from those we instruct.

Be willing to ask for help. Whether you pray or seek, let life show you its abundance. Ask.

Whenever we follow in the path of our beliefs, we will discover more richness than we could ever seek or ask for.

Find new ways to do the best work for the common good. Success is the result of doing whatever has to be done.

Month _____ THE WEEK OF _____ TO _____

	SUNDAY	MONDAY	TUESDAY	WEDNESDAY
MORNING			*A*lways and in everything let there be reverence. CONFUCIUS	
NOON				
AFTERNOON		*T*he measure of a civilization is the degree of its obedience to the unenforceable. LORD MOULTON		*W*hat does rain taste like? SARAH MIDORI ZIMMERMAN
EVENING	*I*deals become starchy habits. CARL JUNG			
GRACE NOTES	*W*hat are your goals for the week? Think noble thoughts and one good, noble thing will lead to another.	*W*e do certain things automatically because we believe they are right. What is a matter of personal honor to you?	*O*ur attitude constitutes all the difference between the perfunctory and the sacred. Revere everything today. Bliss follows.	*W*hen was the last time you took a walk in the rain?

THURSDAY	FRIDAY	SATURDAY	
	All things are changed, and we change with them. LOTHAIR I		*Philosophy* has the task and the opportunity of helping banish the concept that human destiny here and now is of slight importance in comparison with some supernatural destiny. JOHN DEWEY
All the arts are essentially one. JOHN LA FARGE		*Knowledge* of the possible is the beginning of happiness. GEORGE SANTAYANA	THE BEST THINGS THAT HAPPENED THIS WEEK: ....
			GOALS FOR NEXT WEEK: ➷............................... .... ➷............................... ....
Everything can inspire if it is essentially beautiful. Live the art spirit; it is one.	*Everything* is constantly changing. We can improve our lives every day. Respect the past; live in the present.	*Opportunities* for great achievement present themselves every day. Think positively of all you want to accomplish. Just do it and be happy.	*Make* a point of finding meaning and purpose in your life. What are your gifts? How will you use them?

	*S*UNDAY	*M*ONDAY	*T*UESDAY	*W*EDNESDAY
MORNING	*H*e who weighs his responsibilities can bear them. MARTIAL			
NOON		*W*e all like people who do things. WILLA CATHER		
AFTERNOON				*W*e think in generalities, but we live in detail. ALFRED NORTH WHITEHEAD
EVENING			*O*riginality is simply a new pair of eyes. THOMAS WENTWORTH HIGGINSON	
GRACE NOTES	*R*esponsibility means being accountable, dependable and independent. Embrace your responsibilities.	*E*veryone who achieves some recognition has worked hard. Committed, passionate people inspire us with their energy.	*T*oday, look and *really* see every object in your bedroom, bath and kitchen. When we see life uniquely, we will express originality at home.	*D*etails add up to wholeness. Pay careful attention to every detail. Details are the building blocks of beauty.

THURSDAY	FRIDAY	SATURDAY	
		Secure, whate'er he gives, he gives the best. SAMUEL JOHNSON	*A man without decision can never be said to belong to himself.* JOHN FOSTER

Good is not good, where better is expected.
THOMAS FULLER

THE BEST THINGS THAT HAPPENED THIS WEEK:

....
....
....
....
....
....
....

Fortune favors the brave.
TERENCE

**G O A L S
F O R   N E X T   W E E K:**

❧...
....
....
....
❧...
....
....

Do the best you can, no matter what the task. Satisfaction comes from going the extra mile. Expect excellence.

Whenever we are courageous, we are given the strength to overcome obstacles. Bravery builds and prepares you to take more risks.

Give your all. Don't hold back.

Live choicefully. Know what is right for you and what isn't. You will never feel serenity unless you are able to make choices without guilt.

INSPIRATIONS

Take your own life, every one of you.

EDITH WHARTON

What are some of the most inspiring things that have happened to you these past three months? Have you embarked on a new, exciting voyage? Remember, there is no one path. Each one of us is capable of exploring ways to live with more grace, joy and love. What are you most passionate about right now? What thrills you?

Our life is made up of moments. Cumulatively, what we do to fill our time, how we approach each day, what we do to carve out some solitude for reflection, private pleasures and delights makes up a life. Think of this book of days as your story, broken up into chapters and parts. You are living the story and recording it. We are all authors, creators of our own reality.

What are you reading that exhilarates you? Who are some of your favorite authors? What are you most excited about studying now? I'm reading the Fifth Edition of the *Columbia Encyclopedia*. I'm stunned at my ignorance and thrilled to expand my horizons.

What are the things you were once crazy about? Take up something you have put aside in the rush of life; seek continuity. Engage in projects that are yours alone. Stamp collecting, painting, writing poetry, or bird watching will bring a spark of joy when rediscovered.

Who have you heard lecture or perform that inspired you to live more deeply? I cried with joy watching Sam Waterston act in *Abe Lincoln in Illinois*. When was the last time you were so swept away that you had an almost out-of-body experience, forgetting time and place?

What do you do that puts you in the flow of life, that fills you with joy and a sense of love, peace and contentment?

Month _____ THE WEEK OF _____ TO _____

	SUNDAY	MONDAY	TUESDAY	WEDNESDAY
MORNING			*H*ealth is the thing that makes you feel that now is the best time of the year. FRANKLIN P. ADAMS	
NOON	*I* believe in an ultimate decency of things. ROBERT LOUIS STEVENSON			
AFTERNOON		*T*he poet should prefer probable impossibilities to improbable possibilities. ARISTOTLE		
EVENING				*P*hilosophy is nothing but discretion. JOHN SELDEN
GRACE NOTES	*D*on't lose faith. Stay on your path and do everything with a sense of decency and fairness. Live like a poet.	*T*he poet is attracted to seeing the possibilities in the impossibilities.	*A* quick mental health tip: The more you absorb yourself in each day, each season, the more vibrant you will be.	*W*e all have to develop a point of view about life, set limits and commit ourselves to pursue the good. Be a truth seeker.

THURSDAY	FRIDAY	SATURDAY	
		It is life near the bone where it is sweetest. THOREAU	*Seize* this very minute. What you can do or dream, you can begin it. Boldness has genius, power and magic in it. GOETHE
			THE BEST THINGS THAT HAPPENED THIS WEEK: ....
	Audacity, more audacity, and always audacity. DANTON		
For if the talent or individuality is there, it should be expressed. SHIRLEY MACLAINE			GOALS FOR NEXT WEEK: ~ .... ~ ....
What is burning inside you that you want to bring to life? Don't wait for an ideal time. Begin today to express something unique.	*Be* bold. Express your style. Wear brightly colored stockings. Or sprightly ties.	*The* more I simplify, the more pleasure I feel. Learn the art of NO. Practice it regularly. Simplicity is blessed.	*I* love starting something new, not having any idea where it will lead me. Feel the power and magic of boldness.

Month _____ THE WEEK OF _____ TO _____

	SUNDAY	MONDAY	TUESDAY	WEDNESDAY
MORNING	*W*hat I tell you three times is true. LEWIS CARROLL			*S*pend all you have for loveliness. SARA TEASDALE
NOON			*N*ot too much zeal. TALLEYRAND	
AFTERNOON				
EVENING		*T*he secret to writing is writing. WRITERS' BOOT CAMP		
GRACE NOTES	*B*e consistent in purpose and instructions. Repeat for emphasis and emotional impact. Say "I love you" and "Thank you" often.	*W*riters write. It's more than discipline or habit. It is a need, like breathing. The more you write, the more content you are.	*R*emain open to new ideas. Embrace with an open mind.	*B*eauty is priceless. Enduring beauty is a form of immortality. No effort or sacrifice is wasted when you create loveliness.

THURSDAY	FRIDAY	SATURDAY	

A happy life must be to a great extent a quiet life, for it is only in an atmosphere of quiet that true joy can live.

BERTRAND RUSSELL

THE BEST THINGS THAT HAPPENED THIS WEEK:

....
....
....
....
....
....
....

*F*or every disciplined effort there is a multiple reward.

JIM ROHN

*T*he fusion of energy between the audience and the performer is God.

AGNES DE MILLE

GOALS
FOR NEXT WEEK:

....
....
....
....
....
....
....

*C*haracter is higher than intellect.   EMERSON

*W*hen you stretch your envelope, work *really* hard, rewards usually follow. The secret is to see something through to the end. Press on.

*T*here are many intelligent people who, unhappily, are corrupt. Value people you can trust, who have good character above all else.

*W*hat was the last stunning performance you saw? Did you feel the energy?

*H*appiness requires balance among tension, quiet and grace.

Month _____ THE WEEK OF _____ TO _____

	SUNDAY	MONDAY	TUESDAY	WEDNESDAY
MORNING	*No* act of kindness, no matter how small, is ever wasted. AESOP			
NOON		*Rhythm* provides the cadence of life. PETER MEGARGEE BROWN		
AFTERNOON			*Never* tell your resolutions beforehand. JOHN SELDEN	
EVENING				*He* gives twice who gives soon. PUBLILIUS SYRUS
GRACE NOTES	*The* smallest thing you do to show you care holds great power. Act on every impulse to love.	*When* we stay in the natural flow of time we feel balanced and in harmony. Feel your rhythm. Never rush.	*Talk* is easier than action. Better move in the direction of your goals privately. Telling doesn't necessarily help.	*A* short thank-you note is better than a long, delayed letter full of excuses. Be an earth angel and give soon.

THURSDAY

FRIDAY

SATURDAY

The room is full of you!
EDNA ST. VINCENT MILLAY

The happiest people in this world are those who have the most interesting thoughts.
WILLIAM LYON PHELPS

We two form a multitude.
OVID

THE BEST THINGS THAT
HAPPENED THIS WEEK:

....
....
....
....
....
....
....

Appreciation is yeast, lifting ordinary to extraordinary.
MARY-ANN PETRO

GOALS
FOR NEXT WEEK:

....
....
....
....
....
....
....

Look around you at all the remarkable wonders in your midst: the sunrise, the sunset, a child, a flower. Appreciate what you have.

When two people find their other halves, their love can inspire everyone around them. Grow in strength and light together.

Spaces speak of their occupants. Let your rooms radiate your essence, your grace and your love.

When we are able to amuse ourselves with fresh insights and ideas, we are never bored. Happiness is a result of exploring your mind.

	SUNDAY	MONDAY	TUESDAY	WEDNESDAY
MORNING				
NOON			*L* earn that the present hour alone is man's. SAMUEL JOHNSON	
AFTERNOON	*A* ll good things which exist are the fruits of originality. JOHN STUART MILL			*E* very new adjustment is a crisis in self-esteem. ERIC HOFFER
EVENING		*S* orrow and silence are strong, and patient endurance is godlike. LONGFELLOW		
GRACE NOTES	*E* very fresh thought forges new trails. Dare to explore new territory and make it your own.	*W* e learn to be courageous from those who suffer yet never complain.	*D* on't let anyone rob you of your present hour. Put this time to wise use that will bring lasting results and satisfactions.	*T* hink of a new situation as a challenge. How can you help someone else to get through a transition smoothly?

THURSDAY	FRIDAY	SATURDAY	
I bend but do not break. JEAN DE LA FONTAINE			*C*an anyone understand how it is to have lived in the White House, and then, suddenly, to be living alone as the President's widow? JACQUELINE KENNEDY

| | *T*he half is greater than the whole. HESIOD | | THE BEST THINGS THAT HAPPENED THIS WEEK:

....
....
....
....
....
....
.... |

| | | *K*nowledge is a fine thing. MOLIÈRE | GOALS FOR NEXT WEEK:

❧......................................
....
....
....
❧......................................
....
.... |

| *W*e must remain flexible and agile in all matters. Bend. You won't crack; you will remain whole. | *C*ut back. Simplify. Be selective in all you take in and take on. No one gets it all. Half can literally make you whole. | *L*earning keeps us curious, young and vital. What are you studying up on now? What do you find fascinating? | *F*ew of us can understand another's life. Tragedy and sudden loss can happen to any of us. Sympathize. Empathize. |

	SUNDAY	MONDAY	TUESDAY	WEDNESDAY
MORNING	*Envy is a kind of praise.* JOHN JAY			
NOON				*Mount, mount, my soul!* SHAKESPEARE
AFTERNOON		*All greatness is unconscious.* THOMAS CARLYLE		
EVENING			*All are needed by each one; Nothing is fair or good alone.* EMERSON	
GRACE NOTES	*What have you done that is worthy of envy?*	*The wisest, most talented people are often the most humble. Use naturally all God gave you.*	*We need each other. Think of all the people who add richness to your life. Who has helped you the most? We're all intertwined.*	*Think of your life's journey as a lightness of being. We can shed the weights that bog us down, the stress and strains of the ego.*

THURSDAY

I live and love in God's peculiar light.   MICHELANGELO

*B*e a light-seeker and a light-bearer. Envision a candle burning brightly in the center of your being. Spread the radiance.

FRIDAY

A snow year, a rich year.   GEORGE HERBERT

*C*laude Monet loved to paint snow scenes as well as abundant gardens. Bless the four seasons.

SATURDAY

*T*rust your heart.   JUDY COLLINS

*Y*our feelings never lie. Pay attention to the tugs. Think of angels and act as one. Heartfelt actions are angelic.

---

*L*ife here and now would be all right if only you looked at it a little differently.   GEORGE ORWELL

THE BEST THINGS THAT HAPPENED THIS WEEK:

....
....
....
....
....
....
....

GOALS
FOR NEXT WEEK:

....
....
....
....
....
....
....

*B*y changing our attitude and perspective we can create epiphanies in the least likely places. Dwell on life's possibilities.

	SUNDAY	MONDAY	TUESDAY	WEDNESDAY
MORNING		Saying is one thing, and doing is another. MONTAIGNE		
NOON			I saw and loved. EDWARD GIBBON	
AFTERNOON				Excellent things are rare. PLATO
EVENING	In goodness there are all kinds of wisdom. EURIPIDES			
GRACE NOTES	It is always wise to be good. Express your goodness in your own way, on your own terms. When you're good, you're always right.	When I was younger I promised. Now, I do my best. Be a doer, silently.	What have you seen recently that left you in awe? True love is sacred, beautiful and true. Look, realize and love.	Everyone is not equal in their ability to be excellent. We can all be good, and that's all that matters.

THURSDAY

*T*o think is to live. CICERO

FRIDAY

*W*hatever is worth doing at all, is worth doing well.
LORD CHESTERFIELD

SATURDAY

*W*here there is charity and wisdom, there is neither fear nor ignorance.
ST. FRANCIS OF ASSISI

*T*here is always hope for an individual who stops to do some serious thinking about life.
KATHERINE LOGAN

THE BEST THINGS THAT HAPPENED THIS WEEK:

....
....
....
....
....
....
....

GOALS
FOR NEXT WEEK:

....
....
....
....
....
....
....

*Y*ou have power over your own thoughts. The quality of what you think determines the quality of your life. Think lofty thoughts.

*D*oing anything worthwhile requires time and patience. When we enjoy what we're doing, we shed stress and satisfaction abounds.

*F*ear comes from lack of faith in life's basic goodness. Make an effort to give back to the world and fear will go away.

*L*ife requires serious reflection. The more you think, the deeper your journey.

$\mathcal{M}$onth _____ THE WEEK OF _____ TO _____

	$\mathcal{S}$UNDAY	$\mathcal{M}$ONDAY	$\mathcal{T}$UESDAY	$\mathcal{W}$EDNESDAY
MORNING		$\mathcal{L}$ife makes great demands on people's characters. IVY COMPTON-BURNETT		
NOON			$\mathcal{T}$ake up, read! Take up, read! ST. AUGUSTINE	
AFTERNOON	$\mathcal{T}$he secret of success is constancy of purpose. BENJAMIN DISRAELI			$\mathcal{T}$he only reward of virtue is virtue. EMERSON
EVENING				
GRACE NOTES	$\mathcal{E}$veryone who has fire in their bellies will find their purpose. Once you determine it, stick with your vision.	$\mathcal{W}$e are all tempted at times to do something we would not be proud of. Remember, character is also built by saying NO.	$\mathcal{R}$eading books written by wise men is the best tutoring there is. Sunshine, books and flowers bring joy.	$\mathcal{T}$he good we do feels good. The award, the prize, is to be useful to others, using our unique talents. Reward yourself.

THURSDAY	FRIDAY	SATURDAY	
		It matters not how a man dies, but how he lives. SAMUEL JOHNSON	*I find the great thing in this world is not so much where we stand, as in what direction we are moving.* OLIVER WENDELL HOLMES
	If you wish to draw tears from me, you must first feel pain yourself.　HORACE		**THE BEST THINGS THAT HAPPENED THIS WEEK:** ....
A man he seems of cheerful yesterdays. WORDSWORTH			**GOALS FOR NEXT WEEK:** ❧.. .... ❧.. ....
We wear our dispositions on our faces. Cheerfulness is a habit; cultivate it. People will be attracted to you.	*We are far more capable of hurting ourselves than others. When we are angry, we are the anger's first victim.*	*People spend precious time thinking about life after death. I'm far more interested in this life. Live while you're alive.*	*Everything builds. By our daily actions we welcome a fulfilling future. We are not defined by our present situation but by our vision.*

	$\mathscr{S}$UNDAY	$\mathscr{M}$ONDAY	$\mathscr{T}$UESDAY	$\mathscr{W}$EDNESDAY
MORNING			$\mathscr{E}$verything flows. HERACLITUS	
NOON	$\mathscr{L}$ife is not living, but living in health. MARTIAL			
AFTERNOON		$\mathscr{A}$ll who joy would win/ Must share it,—Happiness was born a twin. BYRON		
EVENING				$\mathscr{W}$hen one is pretending the entire body revolts. ANAÏS NIN
GRACE NOTES	$\mathscr{W}$e can work on our wellness by allowing serenity into our lives. Meditate and exercise.	$\mathscr{R}$each out to give a love pat. Take a walk together. Share a sunset. Hold hands. Star gaze.	$\mathscr{E}$verything is moving. Point it in the direction of your dreams. Then, go with the flow. But first, dream big dreams.	$\mathscr{W}$henever we are untrue to ourselves and our nature, there is stress to our immune system. The body always knows.

THURSDAY

FRIDAY

SATURDAY

*B*elieve and succeed.
NORMAN VINCENT PEALE

*H*e who controls others may be powerful, but he who has mastered himself is mightier still.

LAO-TZU

*F*or this relief, much thanks.
SHAKESPEARE

THE BEST THINGS THAT
HAPPENED THIS WEEK:

....
....
....
....
....
....
....

*Y*ou must do the things you think you cannot do.
ELEANOR ROOSEVELT

GOALS
FOR NEXT WEEK:

....
....
....
....
....
....
....

*W*henever something awful happens, we think the pain will last forever. Remember to be thankful when you're given the grace of relief.

*D*on't listen to anyone who says you can't do something. All anything takes is concentration, dedication and luck.

*W*hen you believe in yourself and do your best, success follows. Have faith in what your heart dictates.

*P*eople who live in harmony with themselves have no need to control others. We should all work on ourselves.

	SUNDAY	MONDAY	TUESDAY	WEDNESDAY
MORNING		*Every man is eloquent once in his life.* EMERSON		*I accept the universe!* MARGARET FULLER
NOON			*All good things are cheap; all bad are very dear.* THOREAU	
AFTERNOON				
EVENING	*A single sunbeam is enough to drive away many shadows.* ST. FRANCIS OF ASSISI			
GRACE NOTES	Be a ray of light in a dark corner of the universe. A smile, an encouraging word, an invitation or a letter spread joy.	There are times when we are unusually articulate. Write down your thoughts. What has brought on this clarity?	Have you noticed that the things that give you pleasure cost you nothing?	Acceptance is essential in a well-adapted person. By embracing the universe we expand our potential. Think globally and be accepting.

THURSDAY	FRIDAY	SATURDAY	

*T*o have lived without glory, without leaving a trace of one's existence, is not to have lived at all.

NAPOLEON

*W*hen you're finished changing, you're finished.

BENJAMIN FRANKLIN

THE BEST THINGS THAT
HAPPENED THIS WEEK:

....
....
....
....
....
....
....

*T*he soul is for the most part outside the body.　　JUNG

*T*oo kind—too kind.

FLORENCE NIGHTINGALE

GOALS
FOR NEXT WEEK:

❧..
....
....
....
❧..
....
....

*W*e don't have to know how or where the soul operates. What matters is that we acknowledge the need to nourish our soul.

*R*ecognition for heoric performance often comes late, if at all. Be grateful for having been given the opportunity. The reward is in the doing.

*C*hange is growth. Check yourself regularly to be sure you haven't frozen yourself in a time warp.

*G*lory and triumph require vision, discipline and luck. How do you envision the trace you'll leave of your existence?

	SUNDAY	MONDAY	TUESDAY	WEDNESDAY
Month _____	THE WEEK OF _____ TO _____			

	SUNDAY	MONDAY	TUESDAY	WEDNESDAY
MORNING	The superfluous, a very necessary thing. VOLTAIRE			
NOON				Time and chance happeneth to them all. ECCLESIASTES 9:11
AFTERNOON		The world is large, but in us it is deep as the sea. RAINER MARIA RILKE		
EVENING			Every man is like the company he keeps. LORD CHESTERFIELD	
GRACE NOTES	A little luxury may be a necessary extra. Porcelain, flowers, perfume, wine, embroidery, crystal and silver are enhancements of living.	We contain the world inside us. As individuals we see and experience its depth in a personal way. How large and how deep is your world?	The people around us influence us. The better the company, the more you learn and grow. Surround yourself with superior people.	All of us experience our own journey. We think we are alone but everyone travels the same route.

I expect I shall be a student to the end of my days.

CHEKHOV

Come to the edge, he said. They said, We are afraid. Come to the edge, he said. They came. He pushed them…and they flew.

APOLLINAIRE

Hear the other side.

LORD CHESTERFIELD

THE BEST THINGS THAT
HAPPENED THIS WEEK:

....
....
....
....
....
....
....

Our life is frittered away by detail. Simplify, simplify.

THOREAU

GOALS
FOR NEXT WEEK:

❧ ....
....
....
....
❧ ....
....
....

I usually carry a tote bag full of books, notebooks and clippings. Wherever I go, I'm stimulated and excited about what's around the corner.

Constant activity? When will we ever find real peace? Be selective in your activities. Simplify.

There are more than two sides to everything. Open up to what I have to tell you. I want to hear your view. Tell me.

Why are we so afraid of the unknown? When we dare, we often discover a whole new world. Challenge yourself to do something noble.

	SUNDAY	MONDAY	TUESDAY	WEDNESDAY
MORNING	To know and not to do is not yet to know. ZEN SAYING			
NOON			Love him, or leave him alone! WORDSWORTH	
AFTERNOON				A wise man never loses anything if he has himself. MONTAIGNE
EVENING		The doors of wisdom are never shut. BENJAMIN YOUNG		
GRACE NOTES	Only when we act do we show that we know. Aristotle taught active virtue. Act on truth.	Be a sponge. Open new doors wherever you go. Wisdom comes in the cracks, when you are exploring.	If you can't be loving, kind, sweet and generous, be silent. No one wants or needs to hear anything nasty. Nag not or go.	We will never be able to please everyone. Life is not a popularity contest. Be true to what you hold dear.

THURSDAY   FRIDAY   SATURDAY

Certain gestures made in childhood seem to have eternal repercussions.

ANAÏS NIN

The hole and the patch should be commensurate.
THOMAS JEFFERSON

THE BEST THINGS THAT HAPPENED THIS WEEK:

....
....
....
....
....
....
....

A moment's insight is sometime's worth a life's experience.
OLIVER WENDELL HOLMES

A letter is a deliberate and written conversation.
BALTASAR GRACIÁN

GOALS FOR NEXT WEEK:

....
....
....
....
....
....
....

Don't make a bigger deal out of something than it is. We should try not to exaggerate; deal with the reality.

Suddenly we have a flash of illumination that clarifies everything. Be alert to what Virginia Woolf called "a moment of being."

I'm able to say things in a letter I might never be able to say in conversation. Write a letter and communicate your feelings.

Things we experienced when we were young affect our entire lives. Sift through those memories and concentrate on the positive ones.

Month _____ THE WEEK OF _____ TO _____

	*S*UNDAY	*M*ONDAY	*T*UESDAY	*W*EDNESDAY
MORNING		*O*ne is not born a genius, one becomes a genius. SIMONE DE BEAUVOIR		
NOON	*N*othing is more revealing than movement. MARTHA GRAHAM			
AFTERNOON				*P*erfection belongs to an imaginary world. THOMAS MOORE
EVENING			*B*odies never lie. AGNES DE MILLE	
GRACE NOTES	*W*hen is the last time you danced? Dancing is so freeing. Think of yourself as a dancer and revel in graceful movement.	*O*ur brain is akin to a muscle and needs exercise. Use it or lose it.	*T*aking good care of ourselves requires being aware of the changes that occur gradually. Minor adjustments can prevent illness.	*I*'ve changed my attitude about perfection. Its attainability is a myth that keeps us from our goals. No person or thing is perfect.

THURSDAY	FRIDAY	SATURDAY	
		*S*ome natural sorrow, loss, or pain/That has been, and may be again. WORDSWORTH	*Y*es, if you want to say that I was a drum major, say that I was a drum major for justice; say that I was a drum major for peace; I was a drum major for righteousness. MARTIN LUTHER KING, JR.
*F*aith is the substance of things hoped for, the evidence of things not seen. HEBREWS 11:1			**THE BEST THINGS THAT HAPPENED THIS WEEK:** ....
	*I*t is possible to go wrong in many ways, but right in only one. ARISTOTLE		
			GOALS FOR NEXT WEEK: ....
*T*he more I explore the mystery, the deeper I grow in faith. We will never fully understand. Faith is our ladder to immortality.	*T*here are endless opportunities to mess up. Trust your instincts, and you'll always *know* right from wrong.	*W*hy is it that people who have been through the most difficulty are healers? Life experiences make us courageous or cowards.	*W*hat cause compels you to beat your drum? Is it hunger or education? Is it ecology or wellness? Focus on your passionate concerns next week.

Month _____ THE WEEK OF _____ TO _____

	*S*UNDAY	*M*ONDAY	*T*UESDAY	*W*EDNESDAY
MORNING			*M* an is what he believes. CHEKHOV	
NOON	*I* am a man, I count nothing human indifferent to me. LORD CHESTERFIELD			
AFTERNOON		*W* e must preserve our right to think and differ. ELEANOR ROOSEVELT		
EVENING				*N* o cross, no crown. WILLIAM PENN
GRACE NOTES	*B* y embracing life, we expand our consciousness. By taking everything seriously, we find "divinities in disguise" everywhere.	*R* especting the opinions of others who think and have different views is stimulating. What's crucial is to *really* believe in what you espouse.	*W* e form ourselves by our beliefs. In order to be authentic we have to find our own way, believing some things and disbelieving others.	*W* hoever fed us the fantasy that life has a happy ending? Life is hard work and struggle. The more courageous you are, the happier you become.

	SUNDAY	MONDAY	TUESDAY	WEDNESDAY
MORNING	The first of earthly blessings, independence. — EDWARD GIBBON			
NOON			Art is long and time is fleeting. — LONGFELLOW	
AFTERNOON		We love being in love, that's the truth. — THACKERAY		
EVENING				It is part of the cure to wish to be cured. — SENECA
GRACE NOTES	Being self-sufficient is a powerful, freeing accomplishment. Love follows.	Being in love is a state of consciousness. We see and feel with a new awareness, a fresh appreciation. This week, *live in love.*	Creativity fluctuates. When you are in the flow of your art, give it your full force. "Time is fleeting."	Envision a pain-free, healthy body and heart. Never dwell on illness. Hide your prescriptions from view. Don't allow pity.

THURSDAY

*N*othing is my last word about anything.   HENRY JAMES

FRIDAY

*I*n solitude alone can he know true freedom.
MONTAIGNE

SATURDAY

*M*en willingly believe what they wish.   JULIUS CAESAR

*T*he purpose of life is not to be happy. The purpose of life is to matter, to be productive, to have it make some difference that you live at all.   LEO ROSTEN

THE BEST THINGS THAT HAPPENED THIS WEEK:

....
....
....
....
....
....
....

GOALS
FOR NEXT WEEK:

....
....
....
....
....
....
....

*I*nsights are fluid. As we mature, we embrace a fresh point of view. We're free to change our minds.

*U*ntil we can embrace solitude without loneliness, we aren't free. Value inner resources as a great and noble virtue.

*N*o intelligent, independent person embraces anything 100%. What we believe is private and can only be shared with our higher power.

*H*appiness is the result of pursuing your goals. Increase your usefulness. Happy?

THURSDAY

FRIDAY

The only gift is a portion of thyself. EMERSON

SATURDAY

For what is Mysticism? ...Is it not merely a hard word for "the kingdom of heaven is within"? Heaven is neither a place nor a time. FLORENCE NIGHTINGALE

THE BEST THINGS THAT HAPPENED THIS WEEK:

....
....
....
....
....
....
....

Don't look back. Something might be gaining on you. SATCHEL PAIGE

No one is free who commands not himself. EPICTETUS

**G O A L S
FOR NEXT WEEK:**

....
....
....
....
....
....
....

Just do your best. This is all that we should ever expect from ourselves. Then let go. Believe in yourself and don't worry.

When we sincerely reach out, our gift is our vulnerability. Don't be afraid of rejection. Reach out.

Take your eyes off the other people in your life. Focus on yourself, only.

All the beauty, wonder and majesty you envision is where you are. God is not playing hide and seek. Heaven is already within.

INSIGHTS

It is not enough to stay busy. So, too, are the ants.
The question is what you are busy about.

—HENRY DAVID THOREAU

Half of the year is now over. Look back and analyze the content of your days—work, family, responsibilities, friends. What have been some of your best moments? Who were you with? Why?

The point is not simply to fill up your days. Benjamin Disraeli reminds us that "action may not always bring happiness, but there is no happiness without action." We must also raise the quality of each moment. When you rush about, scattered and exhausted, you are bound to be disappointed. Why wouldn't you be? We are often overambitious about how much we can take on, and therefore fall prey to unrealistic expectations.

Far better to simplify your schedule. Free yourself from self-imposed obligations and unwarranted responsibilities in order to take time to think about the meaning of your journey. Who are the people who enhance your life? What are the things that fulfill you rather than fill up time? What proportion of your time do you spend on your own activities, independent of a boss or a spouse or children? You may think that you should do more, when, in fact, you should be cutting back, readjusting your schedule to provide time for grace notes, insights and reflection. Age alone doesn't make us wise. We should engage in thoughtful meditation regularly.

Pay careful attention to the tugs in your soul. Value the time you spend peacefully without others as much as you look forward to true companionship and sharing. What we want is a balance that allows us to live in a state of soulful grace. It's not easy. It is up to you and you alone to clear the clutter from your path. You will never find time if you wait for a free moment. Take it. Seize it.

	SUNDAY	MONDAY	TUESDAY	WEDNESDAY
MORNING	*W*ithout self-confidence we are as babes in the cradle. VIRGINIA WOOLF			*T*he first hour of the morning is the rudder of the day. BEECHER
NOON				
AFTERNOON		*W*hat mighty contests rise from trivial things. ALEXANDER POPE		
EVENING			*D*o what you can, with what you have, where you are. THEODORE ROOSEVELT	
GRACE NOTES	*C*onfidence is the result of awareness and achievement. Self-confidence builds.	*L*et small issues remain small. Before jumping into the fray, ask yourself how important it is.	*G*enius is making things work out. Don't make excuses for the failure to use wisely what you have. Make something of yourself.	*G*ive yourself the first hour every day. Make this a ritual. Look forward to meditating, reading, writing, walking in the quiet of early morning.

THURSDAY

O aching time! O moments
big as years!
                        JOHN KEATS

When we are in pain, we
feel time stretch eternally
before us. Know that it
shall pass.

FRIDAY

D ream lofty dreams and
as you dream so shall you
become.   JAMES ALLEN

I love to daydream.
Before I go to sleep I program
my dreams, thinking lofty
thoughts. Keep a dream
journal and you'll emulate
them.

SATURDAY

W hen I work, I relax.
                        PICASSO

W hen I write, tension and
stress fall away. What work do
you do that soothes your
nerves? Thinking without
acting makes me nervous.

I have never found,
in anything outside of the
four walls of my study, an
enjoyment equal to sitting
at my writing-desk with a
clean page, a new theme,
and a mind awake.
                WASHINGTON IRVING

THE BEST THINGS THAT
HAPPENED THIS WEEK:

....
....
....
....
....
....
....

GOALS
FOR NEXT WEEK:

....
....
....
....
....
....
....

W hat solitary activity
are you passionate about?
Pursue your bliss and you'll
be connected to a universal
energy.

	*S*UNDAY	*M*ONDAY	*T*UESDAY	*W*EDNESDAY
MORNING				*G*enius is the fire that lights itself. ANONYMOUS
NOON			*B*y a small sample we may judge of the whole piece. CERVANTES	
AFTERNOON		*T*he day may dawn when this plight shall be sweet to remember. VIRGIL		
EVENING	*I* am all ears. TROLLOPE			
GRACE NOTES	*W*hen we're alone we should listen to the stirrings of our soul. When we are among others we should be all ears, learning, growing, expanding.	*W*hen you feel you can't face life, toughen up. Be a fighter and life will be more meaningful because you have overcome the hurdle.	*Q*uality is consistent. You can judge someone's character without knowing everything. We often reveal all when we show a portion of ourselves.	*A*re you a self-starter? Do you wait for others to program you or do you take initiative? When an idea is yours, fire will appear.

THURSDAY

We die only once, and for such a long time!   MOLIÈRE

FRIDAY

Character is what you are in the dark.   DWIGHT MOODY

SATURDAY

Spontaneous courage.   NAPOLEON

Happiness? It is an illusion to think that more comfort means more happiness. Happiness comes of the capacity to feel deeply, to enjoy simply, to think freely, to risk life, to be needed.   STORM JAMESON

THE BEST THINGS THAT HAPPENED THIS WEEK:

....
....
....
....
....
....
....

GOALS
FOR NEXT WEEK:

....
....
....
....
....
....
....

We only live once, and for such a short time! Focus on our aliveness, our vital energy, and what we can accomplish here and now.

Strive at all times to be yourself.

We don't know when we'll be called upon to be brave. In acting strong we will tap into renewable energy. Fear not.

Comfort is the reward of death, not life. Don't be fooled by so-called labor-saving devices. Use your body, your hands and your heart.

	SUNDAY	MONDAY	TUESDAY	WEDNESDAY
MORNING		*J*ust warm life… D. H. LAWRENCE		
NOON	*W*hat I cannot love, I overlook. ANAÏS NIN			*The Two Ways:* One is to suffer; the other is to become a professor of the fact that another suffered. KIERKEGAARD
AFTERNOON				
EVENING			*T*he right time is anytime one is so lucky to be alive. HENRY JAMES	
GRACE NOTES	*T*hose whom we love we think about constantly. How many people do you love spiritually? We all hate to be overlooked.	*T*he greatest joy is that cozy feeling we get when we're able to relax at home.	*D*o you ever contemplate why you are lucky enough to be alive? No matter how challenging life is, we can always count our blessings.	*W*e are never alone in our suffering. Look into the eyes of anyone and feel their pain. Offer empathy and understanding.

THURSDAY

We can never go back again, that much is certain.
DAPHNE DU MAURIER

FRIDAY

Laughter is by definition healthy.
DORIS LESSING

SATURDAY

Too busied with the crowded hour to fear to live or die.
EMERSON

He who hath a clear and lively imagination in his mind, may easily produce and utter the same.
MONTAIGNE

THE BEST THINGS THAT HAPPENED THIS WEEK:

....
....
....
....
....
....
....

GOALS
FOR NEXT WEEK:

....
....
....
....
....
....
....

We have to make a conscious effort to live in the present. Understanding our history makes us move forward with vision and balance.

What makes you laugh? I hope many things. Laughter lightens our burdens and helps digestion.

There's time for action and time for contemplation. Do not confuse the two.

By thinking, reading, being curious and maintaining a childlike wonder, we fuel our imaginations. Write down some of your probing thoughts.

	SUNDAY	MONDAY	TUESDAY	WEDNESDAY
MORNING			*A*ccept a miracle. EDWARD YOUNG	
NOON				*O*ne must keep ever present a sense of humor. KATHERINE MANSFIELD
AFTERNOON		*D*reams are the touchstones of our characters. THOREAU		
EVENING	*T*he way of the sage is to act but not to compete. LAO-TZU			
GRACE NOTES	*W*e are not in competition. The way to success is to use our own talents, living up to our potential. This is a tall order.	*P*ay attention to your dreams. They are the keys to your subconscious. Use this real knowledge.	*W*e shouldn't have to be hit over the head to believe in miracles. The birth of a child is enough proof; the telephone another.	*I*t's difficult to spend much time with a person who is sullen. Humor delights us; we are drawn to it.

THURSDAY

A distraction is to avoid the consciousness of the passage of time.

GERTRUDE STEIN

Distractions offer relief from the ordinary patterns of living. Then we want to get going again, refreshed.

FRIDAY

When you come to the end of a perfect day...

CARRIE JACOBS BOND

Describe what you consider a perfect day. Where are you? Who are you with? What are you up to? Can you make it happen?

SATURDAY

Good fences make good neighbors. ROBERT FROST

Everyone feels more comfortable knowing their boundaries. Value others' privacy as you fiercely guard your own.

The growth of wisdom may be gauged accurately by the decline of ill-temper.

NIETZSCHE

THE BEST THINGS THAT HAPPENED THIS WEEK:

....
....
....
....
....
....
....

GOALS
FOR NEXT WEEK:

....
....
....
....
....
....
....

Do you know someone who is incessantly angry? Ill temper is a form of madness. Wisdom requires stability and a healthy attitude. Think wisely.

Month _____   THE WEEK OF _____ TO _____

	SUNDAY	MONDAY	TUESDAY	WEDNESDAY
MORNING				*S*ing away sorrow, cast away care. CERVANTES
NOON	*W*ise men talk because they have something to say. PLATO		*T*o laugh is proper to man. RABELAIS	
AFTERNOON				
EVENING		*E*very sin is more injury to him who does than to him who suffers it. ST. AUGUSTINE		
GRACE NOTES	*I*t's not how much you say or how often, but what you think that matters. Wise people's conversation enhances our journey.	*T*o sin is to be off the path. Whenever someone is involved in any wrongdoing, they suffer. Pity those who are off their paths.	*L*aughter is always pleasurable. Laugh to cure your blues.	*S*ing in exaltation. While you sing, you celebrate. Let's sing together.

THURSDAY

*F*riendship needs a certain parallelism of life, a community of thought.
HENRY ADAMS

FRIDAY

*L*ove is love's reward.
JOHN DRYDEN

SATURDAY

*P*eople often grudge others what they cannot enjoy themselves.
AESOP

*C*reativity comes when we allow our minds to wander freely.
MICHELE MCCORMICK

THE BEST THINGS THAT HAPPENED THIS WEEK:

....
....
....
....
....
....
....

GOALS
FOR NEXT WEEK:

....
....
....
....
....
....
....

*W*e are friends with people because we share experiences, values and life-style. Call a good friend today.

*L*ove is the ultimate feeling. When you love, you give of yourself. Be the loving one and experience rewards.

*S*hare in a friend's joy and success. What they like is about *them,* not about you.

*E*verything is raw material to be molded and brought forth into a unique artistic expression. Look at everything with an open mind. Seek and be daring.

Month _____ THE WEEK OF _____ TO _____

	SUNDAY	MONDAY	TUESDAY	WEDNESDAY
MORNING	*A*mbition is destruction; only competence matters. JILL ROBINSON			
NOON		*I* have freed my soul. ST. BERNARD		
AFTERNOON				*T*he work and the man are one. CARLOTTA MONTEREY O'NEILL
EVENING			*O*ne can acquire everything in solitude—except character. STENDAHL	
GRACE NOTES	*W*ork with discipline. Being good at what we choose to do with our talents is what matters. Burnished skill makes you competent.	*T*o feel an inner peace requires contemplation. Outer and inner conflicts abound. Have you made peace with all?	*C*haracter is formed step by small step in company and in solitude. Today use solitude to dream.	*N*ext to the word love, work is my favorite. We all do jobs in order to eat. Work is what we do to express ourselves.

*M*ake haste slowly.
SUETONIUS

*S*omeday I hope to enjoy enough of what the world calls success so that someone will ask me: "What's the secret of it?" I shall say simply this: "I get up when I fall down."
PAUL HARVEY

THE BEST THINGS THAT
HAPPENED THIS WEEK:

....
....
....
....
....
....
....

*E*ffort, after days of laziness, seemed impossible.
DORIS LESSING

*D*iscipline—in every way.
BROOKE ASTOR

GOALS
FOR NEXT WEEK:

....
....
....
....
....
....
....

*L*ongevity, leadership and respect are not accidental. Discipline is the linchpin to a successful life. It is the rudder that keeps us on course.

*O*ne of the reasons artists and writers rarely take a day off is because they need to stay at the center of their efforts. Begin.

*M*ove in the direction of your goal. Pace yourself for the finish. Timing, rhythm and ease are key.

*W*hen we were young, our mothers kissed our scratched knees. We were healed. Now we must heal ourselves.

	SUNDAY	MONDAY	TUESDAY	WEDNESDAY
MORNING			*T*ry thinking of love, or something. CRISTOPHER FRY	
NOON	*A*lways to be best, and distinguished above the rest. HOMER			
AFTERNOON				*T*here is no wisdom in useless and hopeless sorrow. SAMUEL JOHNSON
EVENING		*L*ive in this moment and live in eternity. GOETHE		
GRACE NOTES	*E*veryone and everything plays a part in the human drama. Make a real contribution by being excellent. Shine.	*L*earn to live in an eternal now-ness. Concentrate on everything you see and do. Now. Now.	*W*e program our minds and hearts. Love is positive. Hate is negative. By thinking of love we become loving. Grace and joy result from loving.	*G*rieving, while unavoidable, must be transformed into strength and wisdom. Excess sorrow is the other side of joy. Choose joy.

THURSDAY

I do not understand;
I pause; I examine.   MONTAIGNE

FRIDAY

*W*hat tranquil joy his
friendly presence gives!
OLIVER WENDELL HOLMES

SATURDAY

*S*ickness need not be a part
of life.   ADELLE DAVIS

*T*he joy of life is
variety; the tenderest love
requires to be renewed by
intervals of absence.
SAMUEL JOHNSON

THE BEST THINGS THAT
HAPPENED THIS WEEK:

....
....
....
....
....
....
....

GOALS
FOR NEXT WEEK:

....
....
....
....
....
....
....

*E*veryone seems in a rush for
the answer. Who takes time to
examine the questions? We're
not born wise.

*W*hich of your friends
bring you joy by their mere
presence? Just thinking of
them will bring you peace,
contentment and hope.

*T*hink of living a long,
healthy life. Focus on energy,
vitality and optimism. Spread
joy and light. Take care of
your own health. Stay well.

*W*hen I am away from
loved ones, I appreciate their
qualities. When I'm with loved
ones, I enjoy them. Come,
share with me.

Month _____ THE WEEK OF _____ TO _____

	Sunday	Monday	Tuesday	Wednesday
MORNING				*T*hat is the road we all have to take. KIERKEGAARD
NOON				
AFTERNOON		*T*ime is the most valuable thing a man can spend. THEOPHRASTUS		
EVENING	*B*ring equal ease unto my pain. THOMAS CAREW		*L*et all things be done decently and in order. CORINTHIANS	
GRACE NOTES	*L*ife never gives us all pain or all pleasure. We all experience our share of challenges and disappointments as well as celebrations.	*A*t our deaths, we could have a fortune saved up. Time? We can't save it. Spend it well. Live it. Now.	*T*here is a divine order to all things. There is a right timing. What's next?	*O*ur daughter Brooke's metaphor for life is journey. Eliminate negative, poisonous energy along your road. Live.

THURSDAY

The life is short, the craft
so long to learn.   HIPPOCRATES

The sooner we find out
what we're passionate about,
the sooner we can learn our
craft. We then get better at the
art of living.

FRIDAY

One thought fills immensity.

WILLIAM BLAKE

One clear thought may
obliterate twenty years
of muddle. What are you
thinking?

SATURDAY

But above all, try something.

FRANKLIN DELANO ROOSEVELT

Ask yourself, What is the
worst thing that could happen
to you? Life well lived requires
risks. Being afraid to try is a
lost opportunity.

What kind of world
would this be if everybody
in it were just like me?

KANT

THE BEST THINGS THAT
HAPPENED THIS WEEK:

....
....
....
....
....
....
....

GOALS
FOR NEXT WEEK:

❧ ....
....
....
....
❧ ....
....
....

Seek to find your
uniqueness. Express
your fire through color,
cooking, writing or painting.
Who *are* you?

Month _____ THE WEEK OF _____ TO _____

	SUNDAY	MONDAY	TUESDAY	WEDNESDAY
MORNING	*The* reason of the strongest is always the best. JEAN DE LA FONTAINE			
NOON			*But* I have promises to keep/And miles to go before I sleep. ROBERT FROST	
AFTERNOON				*Tis* always morning somewhere in the world. RICHARD HENRY HORNE
EVENING		*Life* is the childhood of our immortality. GOETHE		
GRACE NOTES	*Hone* your reasoning strengths. Until we can think clearly for ourselves, we will always depend on others.	*Whatever* good you do now will never die. We die; our virtue doesn't.	*We* all have to get going. We've made promises to ourselves as well as to others. There is much we can accomplish before we sleep.	*Sometimes* we don't understand what is happening to us. What we see is not the whole picture. When it's dark, think of the sunshine.

THURSDAY

I believe because it is impossible.   TERTULLIAN

FRIDAY

*T*he time to relax is when you don't have time for it.
                    SYDNEY J. HARRIS

SATURDAY

*E*very day, in every way, I'm growing better and better.
                    ÉMILE COUÉ

A vigorous five-mile walk will do more good for an unhappy but otherwise healthy adult than all the medicine and psychology in the world.
                    PAUL DUDLEY WHITE

THE BEST THINGS THAT
HAPPENED THIS WEEK:

....
....
....
....
....
....
....

GOALS
FOR NEXT WEEK:

....
....
....
....
....
....
....

---

*W*e will never be able to figure everything out. But with faith, we can believe in the possible. Think of what you *can* do.

*T*he more we enjoy our daily activities, the more relaxation we will get from whatever we do. Take time to relax.

*D*o you feel you are continuing to grow and stretch *every* day? When we are learning and acquiring wisdom, we *do* get better.

*E*verything about walking is good for us. We clear our heads, invigorate our bodies and take time out. Let's go for a vigorous walk. Today.

	$\mathcal{S}$UNDAY	$\mathcal{M}$ONDAY	$\mathcal{T}$UESDAY	$\mathcal{W}$EDNESDAY
MORNING			$\mathcal{V}$irtue proceeds through effort. EURIPIDES	
NOON				
AFTERNOON		$\mathcal{I}$t is not good to refuse a gift. HOMER		$\mathcal{E}$ither a beast or a god. ARISTOTLE
EVENING	$\mathcal{T}$hings do not change; we change. THOREAU			
GRACE NOTES	$\mathcal{W}$e become more aware. We see things differently. Growth allows us to reconsider prior opinions. We grow wise as we change. Keep changing.	$\mathcal{N}$ever be embarrassed by a genuine present. Receive it with grace.	$\mathcal{W}$e don't become virtuous automatically. Whenever we make an effort, going the extra mile, we practice active virtue.	$\mathcal{T}$he choice is usually not between two extremes. Practice generosity and kindness and you'll be closer to godliness.

THURSDAY

*L*et there be truth between us two forevermore. EMERSON

FRIDAY

*L*ove, and do what you will. ST. AUGUSTINE

SATURDAY

*L*eisure with dignity. CICERO

*N*o man who continues to add something to the material, intellectual and moral well-being of the place in which he lives is left long without proper reward. BOOKER T. WASHINGTON

THE BEST THINGS THAT HAPPENED THIS WEEK:

....
....
....
....
....
....
....

GOALS
FOR NEXT WEEK:

❧ ....
....
....
....
❧ ....
....
....

*B*e a truth-seeker and a truth-bearer. You cannot control other people but you can face reality. Without truth there is no beauty.

*W*hatever you do, be in a loving frame of consciousness. Everything will then become sacred. Love is all we need.

*T*ake little private holidays. Treat yourself to some relaxed time when you free yourself of obligations. Create space for dignity and grace.

*R*ecognition is apt to follow excellence. Focus on all the modest, simple things you can do to add beauty, grace and joy. Reward yourself.

	SUNDAY	MONDAY	TUESDAY	WEDNESDAY
MORNING	*H*e is well paid that is well satisfied. SHAKESPEARE		*L*et there be light. GENESIS	
NOON		*B*e a friend to yourself, and others will. SCOTTISH PROVERB		
AFTERNOON				
EVENING				*E*very house has a voice. LIZ SEYMOUR
GRACE NOTES	*W*henever we feel fulfilled, we appreciate our lives. Like what you do; money will follow.	*E*very loving act you do for yourself is always translated into loving, generous acts of friendship.	*L*ight a candle, symbol of an eternal flame. The flickering glow warms the heart and expands hope.	*E*very house speaks to us. Some sound sad while others sing out with joy. The difference between a house and a home is a voice.

THURSDAY

*E*xample is always more efficacious than precept.

SAMUEL JOHNSON

FRIDAY

*T*o know that you do not know is the best.   LAO-TZU

SATURDAY

*L*ove is a great beautifier.

LOUISA MAY ALCOTT

I wish you some new love at lovely things/and some new forgetfulness at the teasing things/and some higher pride in the praising things/and some sweeter peace from the hurrying things/and some closer fence from the worrying things.   JOHN RUSKIN

THE BEST THINGS THAT HAPPENED THIS WEEK:

....
....
....
....
....
....
....

GOALS
FOR NEXT WEEK:

❧...
....
....
....
❧...
....
....

*W*e are responsible for our acts and teach by example. Who are your mentors?

*E*ven geniuses have blind spots. Do research. Ask for help. We'll never be bored trying to know more. Help!

*W*hether we love a child, another, or our work, there is a radiance about us that is beautiful. Think about all you love.

I wish you every goodness. I want your dreams to come true. May you soar with your own greatness, expand your essence and feel joy.

	SUNDAY	MONDAY	TUESDAY	WEDNESDAY
MORNING		*A* man of learning has riches within him. PHAEDRUS		
NOON			*I* f you rest, you rust. HELEN HAYES	
AFTERNOON				*W* isdom must be sought. EDWARD YOUNG
EVENING	*P* erform with all your heart your long and heavy task. ALFRED DE VIGNY			
GRACE NOTES	*C* oncentrated effort and determination never hurts us. Quitting too soon, losing focus, giving up break our hearts and ultimately kill us.	*O* ur inner treasures can go wherever we go without fear of theft. Make yourself beautiful with learning.	*K* eep climbing those mountains. We get energy from energy. Keep all your energy circuits lit up. Rest after death.	*Q* uestion everything. Do your own research. Use a variety of sources. Form your own opinions. Believe in your ability to become wise.

THURSDAY

*F*ailure is impossible.
SUSAN B. ANTHONY

FRIDAY

*H*e is most powerful who has power over himself.
SENECA

SATURDAY

*B*etter to light one candle than to curse the darkness.
THE CHRISTOPHERS

*T*he only limit to our realization of tomorrow will be our doubts of today.
FRANKLIN DELANO ROOSEVELT

THE BEST THINGS THAT HAPPENED THIS WEEK:

....
....
....
....
....
....
....

GOALS
FOR NEXT WEEK:

....
....
....
....
....
....
....

*B*roaden your perspective. Have goals that enlarge you and make a difference. Study the lives of your heroes and heroines.

*S*elf-control, self-resolve, self-confidence, self-respect, self-love equal self-power!

*T*he world is full of hopeless, faithless people. Think what you can do to spread light. Find solutions. Inspire a love of life.

*I*t's natural, at times, to be afraid. The more we care, the more vulnerable we are. Never doubt your ability to make your *own* mark.

QUESTS

Life is a quest.

EDNA ST. VINCENT MILLAY

How do you feel about the first three-quarters of your year? This is the final stretch. No day can be repeated. Every act has consequences. Have you done something you're proud of? Have you taken on a project that means a great deal to you? What have been some of your goals? Have you been able to share in some good news of family and friends? How is your health? How is your energy?

No matter how much we identify with a spouse or child or our career, we should remember our own quests. What fills you with hope and what do you want to do in the short time left this year? This is your only lifetime. How intensely are you pursuing your goals?

Have you tried hard enough? When you need help, are you humble? Can you ask for assistance? When you feel discouraged, do you take time to reflect and let the pain teach you new dimensions of courage? Do you renew your faith in life regularly by counting your blessings and appreciating your hard-earned wisdom?

How much do you care about the quality of your daily journey? Do you have a ready smile, a bounce to your step, an enthusiasm about life that is infectious? Are you in control of your time? Do you arrange your schedule so you can thoughtfully pursue your interests, your passions, and increase your self-awareness?

Think of our lives as interconnecting circles. Every link is vital in the chain that binds us together. It is for us to make something of our being placed on earth at the same time. Find the reason. Let your journey through this world bring hope and faith, love and grace to you and those around you.

	SUNDAY	MONDAY	TUESDAY	WEDNESDAY
MORNING				
NOON				Nothing human is foreign to me. TERENCE
AFTERNOON	I am nearer home today than I have ever been before. PHOEBE CARY		It is certain because it is impossible. TERTULLIAN	
EVENING		I must find a way to live more simply. RUTH ST. DENIS		
GRACE NOTES	The essence of who we are becomes clear to us. We become whole and feel at home in our souls. How near home are you?	People clutter up their lives because they haven't found their inner fire. Once we discover our passion, we tend to simplify.	I like people with strong convictions and the fighting instinct to bring something forth. Without this faith, we collapse.	Living requires getting more than our hands dirty. Experience everything yourself. Trust your instincts.

THURSDAY	FRIDAY	SATURDAY	
	To look up is joy. CONFUCIUS		*I* love the man that can smile in trouble, that can gather strength from distress, and grow brave by reflection. THOMAS PAINE
			THE BEST THINGS THAT HAPPENED THIS WEEK: ....
		Any excuse will serve a tyrant. AESOP	
For man is man and master of his fate. TENNYSON			GOALS FOR NEXT WEEK: ❧... .... ❧... ....
You can become as great as you dare try. Death cannot end your power to spread love.	*Take* a deep breath and embrace the world around you.	*You* are in charge. Learn from your mistakes. Grow. Don't blame others. No excuses.	*Being* gloomy never helps a situation. A dying person wants to be cheered up. Grieve, reflect, then be strong and brave. It's okay to smile.

Month _____ THE WEEK OF _____ TO _____

	_S_UNDAY	_M_ONDAY	_T_UESDAY	_W_EDNESDAY
MORNING	_T_o be that self which one truly is. KIERKEGAARD			_V_irtue is its own reward. CICERO
NOON			_H_ear the other side. ST. AUGUSTINE	
AFTERNOON				
EVENING		_N_othing short of independence, it appears to me, can possibly do. GEORGE WASHINGTON		
GRACE NOTES	_P_retension is such a waste of everyone's time. The greater the person, the more genuine and authentic. Being true requires strict limits. Be _you_.	_B_eing free to act according to your beliefs is essential. Dictators come in all sizes and disguises. Don't accept any compromises. Fight.	_L_isten to the pain, the fear, the blindness, the anger as well as the reasoning behind someone's view. Hearing them out can clarify some differences.	_D_oing what's right, no matter how costly or painful, pays off; never compromise yourself out of fear or embarrassment.

THURSDAY	FRIDAY	SATURDAY	
			*O*pportunities are usually disguised as hard work, so most people don't recognize them. ANN LANDERS
		*I*f you are hungry, you're losing weight. PETER MEGARGEE BROWN	**THE BEST THINGS THAT HAPPENED THIS WEEK:** ....
*S*upreme impartiality is antihuman. GEORGE SAND			
	*W*e all die with our secret. BERTHE MORISOT		**GOALS FOR NEXT WEEK:** ....
*T*ake a stand. Cast your vote. Have a point of view. You don't have to be prejudiced to have an opinion. Allow subjectivity. It's honest.	*N*o need to tell all. We're allowed our private thoughts, our personal failures, regrets and longings. It doesn't bring back a loss to tell. Secret!	*D*on't eat unless you're hungry. Your stomach talks. No force-feedings.	*W*e've been tricked as a society to want ease. But opportunities that are easy aren't worth the trouble. Work!

	SUNDAY	MONDAY	TUESDAY	WEDNESDAY
MORNING	*Not angles, but angels.* GREGORY I		*When soul is present, nature is alive.* THOMAS MOORE	
NOON		*It is only to the individual that a soul is given.* ALBERT EINSTEIN		
AFTERNOON				
EVENING				*Praising what is lost makes the remembrance dear.* SHAKESPEARE
GRACE NOTES	*Concentrate on angels. Think with a pure heart. Not everyone is looking for an angle. Become an earth angel. The world craves angels.*	*Believing that there is a reason individuals possess a soul expands our spiritual horizons*	*Soul is the quintessence, the vital life force. Nature is soulful, alive, real, unending. Understand imperishable truth through nature.*	*Celebrating the life of a loved one keeps their spirit alive. Revitalize the life, not the death.*

Month _____ THE WEEK OF _____ TO _____

THURSDAY	FRIDAY	SATURDAY	
			If you would win a man to your cause, first convince him that you are his sincere friend. ABRAHAM LINCOLN
	Hurry is the weakness of fools. BALTASAR GRACIÁN		**THE BEST THINGS THAT HAPPENED THIS WEEK:** ....
I find nothing so dear as that which is given me. MONTAIGNE		*Talent is best nurtured in solitude.* GOETHE	
			GOALS FOR NEXT WEEK: ....
The art of appreciation is a sacred gift. Open up your arms and sing the praises of your many gifts. Hallelujah. Amen.	*Where are we headed? What's the hurry? We become scattered when we rush about. It makes us anxious. Gentle swiftness.*	*When we're constantly hanging around people, we're not able to develop our talent. We nurture potential in solitude.*	*Until we know you really care about us we will not easily be convinced about anything. Most of us are open to a sincere friend's cause.*

	Month _____	THE WEEK OF _____	TO _____	
	*S*UNDAY	*M*ONDAY	*T*UESDAY	*W*EDNESDAY
MORNING				*W*e know the truth, not only by reason, but by the heart. PASCAL
NOON				
AFTERNOON		*W*e are always the same age inside. GERTRUDE STEIN		
EVENING	*W*hat wisdom can you find that is greater than kindness? JEAN-JACQUES ROUSSEAU		*U*ncertainty and expectation are the joys of life. WILLIAM CONGREVE	
GRACE NOTES	*A*ny kindness you experience or extend is grace. Touch a heart with your kindest self.	*N*ow that my daughters are adults, our age difference seems to melt away. We share jewelry, scarves and confidences. Inner agelessness transcends age.	*M*ay your future days be filled with uncertainty so you have the thrill of anticipation and expectation. Let joy fill your days.	*W*hen our heart aches we don't always understand why. But truth tugs at us and forces us to pay attention. Truth is deeply felt.

THURSDAY	FRIDAY	SATURDAY	
		Nothing can be created out of nothing. LUCRETIUS	*Only* in growth, reform and change, paradoxically enough, is true security to be found. ANNE MORROW LINDBERGH
As for me, prizes mean nothing. My prize is my work. KATHARINE HEPBURN			**THE BEST THINGS THAT HAPPENED THIS WEEK:** ....
	Exuberance is beauty. WILLIAM BLAKE		
			GOALS FOR NEXT WEEK: ....
No prize is meaningful unless it is deserved. The work that created the award is the life force. What is your prize? Your work?	*Whatever* you are enthusiastic about will make you beautiful. The more exuberant, the more beautiful.	*Be* active about your desires. Make things happen for you. Send your ship out to sail. And don't be afraid of rejection.	*Why* are we afraid of change? Circumstances are always changing. We must take risks, embrace change.

Month _____ THE WEEK OF _____ TO _____

	SUNDAY	MONDAY	TUESDAY	WEDNESDAY
MORNING		*I* like to be distinguished. MOLIÈRE		*S*peech is the picture of the mind. JOHN KAY
NOON	*I*n the beginning was the word. JOHN			
AFTERNOON				
EVENING			*O*n this whirligig of time we circle with the seasons. TENNYSON	
GRACE NOTES	*S*ince you've grown up, how many of your childhood beliefs have you shed? How much time do you set aside for meditation?	*B*eing accomplished and acclaimed in a specialty feels good. Don't be shy in accepting praise.	*E*verything is a circle. We need to find the connecting links. As the seasons come and go, they teach us faith, hope, love and change.	*W*e communicate our thoughts when we talk and write. Pay attention to your mind. Think beautiful thoughts.

THURSDAY	FRIDAY	SATURDAY	

*E*ach morning see a task begun, each evening see it close. Something attempted, something done, has earned a night's repose.

LONGFELLOW

*W*hat I long for I have.

NARCISSUS

THE BEST THINGS THAT HAPPENED THIS WEEK:

....
....
....
....
....
....
....

*H*onor is simply the morality of superior men.

H. L. MENCKEN

I am independent! I can live alone and I love to work.

MARY CASSATT

GOALS FOR NEXT WEEK:

....
....
....
....
....
....
....

*W*e dignify ourselves when we show proper respect for others. Looking up to certain people elevates our sights.

*F*ew people can claim such freedom. Each of us should be prepared to live alone.

*W*hat are your unmet needs and longings? I feel complete now that we've found our seaside cottage. Do you have what you long for?

*T*here is satisfaction in completion. We need closure to feel accomplishment. Begin one thing each day and finish it before you sleep.

		Month _____ THE WEEK OF _____ TO _____	
	*S*UNDAY	*M*ONDAY	*T*UESDAY	*W*EDNESDAY
MORNING			*N*o man is wise enough by himself. TITUS MACCIUS PLAUTUS	
NOON		*I*t's futile to have regrets. HELENE HANFF		
AFTERNOON				*J*oy is a net of love by which you can catch souls. MOTHER TERESA
EVENING	*T*he two noblest of things…are sweetness and light. JONATHAN SWIFT			
GRACE NOTES	*L*ook for sweet things as well as people. Sweetness is never mean or sour. Light puts a smile on everything. Sweetness and light to you.	*R*egrets are so passive. You can't do anything. Focus on now, what actions you can take. Live with as few regrets as possible.	*T*hink of all your teachers, those grace-bearers in your life who have guided you, encouraged you, loved you and inspired you. Give thanks.	*M*other Teresa persuaded a tearful volunteer to stay by saying, "We're not afraid here; we love and heal."

THURSDAY

FRIDAY

It's later than you think.
WRITING ON A CHINESE WALL

SATURDAY

People are ridiculous only when they try to seem or to be that which they are not.
GIACOMO LEOPARDI

We are always getting ready to live, but never living.
EMERSON

THE BEST THINGS THAT HAPPENED THIS WEEK:

....
....
....
....
....
....
....

In the long run, men only hit what they aim at.
THOREAU

GOALS FOR NEXT WEEK:

....
....
....
....
....
....
....

Jump right in and live now. There will never be a better time. You will never be the same person. Catch life on the fly.

Every day be conscious of the shortness of life and the limits of time. Take nothing for granted. Each day is a precious gift.

Set your sights high. If you do achieve all your goals you will surprise yourself by the joy in your accomplishments. Hit the mark!

Why are people so dissatisfied with themselves? Seek authenticity, honesty and truth. Be that real person you are.

	SUNDAY	MONDAY	TUESDAY	WEDNESDAY
MORNING	*Life* is either a daring adventure or it is nothing. HELEN KELLER			
NOON		*Our* sight is the most perfect and most delightful of all our senses. JOSEPH ADDISON		*Joy* is a flame in me too steady to destroy. SARA TEASDALE
AFTERNOON			*Knowledge* and human power are synonymous. FRANCIS BACON	
EVENING				
GRACE NOTES	*It* requires daring to be yourself. Life isn't for sissies. Live deeply, dare beautifully and enjoy life's adventure.	*Helen* Keller never had sight, yet she brought great insights and guts to bear on her life. Use your eyes to *really* see.	*Be* a student of life. Freedom is earned, not granted. Learn, digest and have power.	*Keep* the flame of joy in your heart. Don't let setbacks, disappointments or world events rob you of your moments of joy. Joy is grace.

THURSDAY	FRIDAY	SATURDAY	
		I am always with myself, and it is I who am my tormentor. TOLSTOI	*Risk! Risk anything! Care no more for the opinions of others, for those voices. Do the hardest thing on earth for you. Act for yourself. Face the truth.* KATHERINE MANSFIELD
			THE BEST THINGS THAT HAPPENED THIS WEEK:
			....
			....
			....
			....
			....
			....
			....
	Faith which does not doubt is dead faith. MIGUEL DE UNAMUNO		
All the pleasure of life is in general ideas. OLIVER WENDELL HOLMES			**GOALS FOR NEXT WEEK:**
			❧..
			....
			....
			....
			❧..
			....
			....
Being interested in all kinds of ideas provides a great deal of pleasure wherever you are. Open yourself up to new interests every day.	*Doubt makes us think. Doubt helps confim our beliefs.*	*How often do you consider who your true companion is? Day, night, weeks, months, years, decades—a lifetime of you. Become your best friend.*	*Life lived fully is a risky adventure. Stretch yourself. Don't wait for approval. Pay no attention to doubting Thomas. Act, risk, dare—live.*

Month _____ THE WEEK OF _____ TO _____

	SUNDAY	MONDAY	TUESDAY	WEDNESDAY
MORNING	*The* he ancestor of every action is a thought. EMERSON			*What* hat I give, I give freely. ELEANOR ROOSEVELT
NOON			*Ye* e immortal gods, where in the world are we? CICERO	
AFTERNOON				
EVENING		. . .*The* he never-ending flight of future days. JOHN MILTON		
GRACE NOTES	*Aristotle* ristotle believed in active virtue. Don't hesitate to follow up on your thoughts. What you think becomes who you are.	*All* ll our days will fly by whether we have anything exciting to record or not. By keeping a journal or a book of days, we magnify time.	*Today* oday the world spins so rapidly. We wonder where we are and where we're going. Pay attention to universal truths and to preserving civilization.	*Never* ever follow a gift. Enjoy the pleasure of giving and let go. Don't cling. Make anonymous donations to charities.

THURSDAY	FRIDAY	SATURDAY	
			*M*y own conviction has always been to seek the inner reality, with the belief that the fruits of future values will be able to grow only after they are sown by the values of our history. ROLLO MAY
		*T*hese things were permanent, they could not be dissolved. DAPHNE DU MAURIER	**THE BEST THINGS THAT HAPPENED THIS WEEK:** ....
	I think, therefore I am. DESCARTES		
A man dishonored is worse than dead. CERVANTES			**GOALS FOR NEXT WEEK:** ❧.................................... .... ❧.................................... ....
*D*on't do anything to dishonor yourself. Character, virtue, integrity, honesty and truth are more sacred than anything else.	*W*e are the essence of our thoughts. Believing in the goodness of our fellow human beings keeps discouragement at bay.	*T*here are a lot of things of value that cannot be replaced. What are the principles most permanent in your life? Faith, hope, truth, love?	*W*e live in our own time. We can only respond responsibly to the reality we experience. Future values, if different, will take care of themselves.

	SUNDAY	MONDAY	TUESDAY	WEDNESDAY
MORNING			*H*eaven from all creatures hides the book of fate. ALEXANDER POPE	
NOON		*E*very beginning is hard. GERMAN PROVERB		
AFTERNOON	*I*n a man's letters his soul lies naked. SAMUEL JOHNSON			
EVENING				*H*e who has begun his task has half done it. Have the courage to be wise. HORACE
GRACE NOTES	*W*hether we write a love letter, a journal, a newspaper column, an essay or a book, we expose our inner selves. Are you willing?	*E*very self-doubt and fear is magnified in the void prior to our beginning. Start today. Greatness builds from a leap of faith and commitment.	*P*eople defuse death's sting by thinking about heaven. Our fate is to die. Can heavenly angels change this reality?	*R*emember there are no pure beginnings. We're already in the throes of things. Just do it. Don't wait until it's impossible. Be wise. Begin.

Month _____ THE WEEK OF _____ TO _____

THURSDAY	FRIDAY	SATURDAY	
		Find your inner light and shine it on others. ELISABETH CAREY LEWIS	*Example is not the main thing in life…it is the only thing.* ALBERT SCHWEITZER
	The essential thing is the life of the individual. JUNG		THE BEST THINGS THAT HAPPENED THIS WEEK: ....
Imagination is more important than knowledge. ALBERT EINSTEIN			
			GOALS FOR NEXT WEEK: ❧............................ .... ❧............................ ....
Don't wait for knowledge to come to you. Imagine situations. Visualize events. Are you a storyteller? What's the scenario?	*When you are concerned enough to take care of yourself, everything else seems to fall into place. This is up to each individual to do.*	*The only true happiness comes from self-illumination that can be shared with others. The more we discover, the more we can give away.*	*Little is learned from hypocrites. We don't gain inspiration from a deceiver or a cheat. Genuinely loving actions light our path.*

Month _____ THE WEEK OF _____ TO _____

	SUNDAY	MONDAY	TUESDAY	WEDNESDAY
MORNING	They can because they think they can. VIRGIL			
NOON		As men, we are all equal in the presence of death. PUBLILIUS SYRUS		Existence is always in process of self-transcending. ROLLO MAY
AFTERNOON				
EVENING			There are two kinds of beauty—loveliness and dignity. CICERO	
GRACE NOTES	My favorite childhood book was *The Little Engine That Could*. Think you can, and you can. "I think I can… I thought I could." Try.	Look into the eyes of a friend or neighbor and understand *their* journey. We are all together here on earth, now and in death.	Loveliness doesn't automatically give one dignity. What respect you have for yourself and are granted by others is high beauty.	We never have to be stuck in a rut. Change can be disquieting, but it always opens doors to growth.

THURSDAY	FRIDAY	SATURDAY	
			*K*eep your fears to yourself but share your courage with others. ROBERT LOUIS STEVENSON
			THE BEST THINGS THAT HAPPENED THIS WEEK: ....
*N*o, I ask it for the knowledge of a lifetime. WHISTLER		*T*he greater man the greater courtesy.　TENNYSON	
	*S*o even in despair, man and woman must laugh. LIN YUTANG		GOALS FOR NEXT WEEK: ....
*C*reative people cannot be properly paid by the hour. What seems to be the result of a burst of inspiration took a lifetime.	*W*e can't take life and our present situation *too* seriously. A little laughter helps ease the pain.	*P*eople who are really accomplished tend to be considerate and generous. Emulate them.	*A*ssume we are all frightened of something. When someone shares a courageous act with us, we are strengthened.

	SUNDAY	MONDAY	TUESDAY	WEDNESDAY
MORNING		*H*e that increaseth knowledge increaseth sorrow. ECCLESIASTES		
NOON	*I*f you want to be happy, be. TOLSTOI		*M*ake yourself necessary to somebody. EMERSON	
AFTERNOON				
EVENING				*B*e sure you are right; then go ahead. DAVID CROCKETT
GRACE NOTES	*W*hat's keeping you from having a marvelous day? Don't let troubles weigh you down. Choose happiness.	*I*n gaining knowledge we learn about pain but also about joy. Choose knowledge.	*W*henever we connect, we assume a responsibility for others. Be accountable and responsive.	*W*henever you research something and believe it is right for you at the time, make a commitment in good faith.

$\mathcal{T}$HURSDAY	$\mathcal{F}$RIDAY	$\mathcal{S}$ATURDAY	
	$\mathcal{V}$ision is the art of seeing things invisible. JONATHAN SWIFT		$\mathcal{W}$hat would you attempt to do if you knew you could not fail? ROBERT SCHULLER

$\mathcal{L}$ove is a force.
ANNE MORROW LINDBERGH

THE BEST THINGS THAT
HAPPENED THIS WEEK:

....
....
....
....
....
....
....

$\mathcal{A}$ teacher affects eternity.
HENRY BROOKS ADAMS

GOALS
FOR NEXT WEEK:

....
....
....
....
....
....
....

$\mathcal{A}$ll of us have power to influence others positively or negatively. Teach truth kindly.

$\mathcal{T}$rue vision requires faith and imagination. Reality is far too complex to comprehend completely. Give in to the mystery.

$\mathcal{D}$on't always insist on being logical, rational and sensible. When you are in the force of love, you will know great power.

$\mathcal{F}$ailure begins with letting fear rule you. Whenever we try, no matter what we attempt, if we stick with it we won't fail. What will you try?

Month _____ THE WEEK OF _____ TO _____

	SUNDAY	MONDAY	TUESDAY	WEDNESDAY
MORNING	First...go to the light. ANTHONY B. PETRO			I don't wish you anything but just what you are—. IBSEN
NOON				
AFTERNOON			Change the name, and the tale is about you. HORACE	
EVENING		It all began so beautifully. LADY BIRD JOHNSON		
GRACE NOTES	Light is glory. As soon as you wake up, get a cup of coffee and go to a window or outside to experience the light.	No one knows what is going to happen. We take risks, do what we believe is right for us and take our chances. Begin beautifully.	Do you identify with others? Imagining ourselves in other people's situations helps us appreciate our own predicament.	Stay as caring and genuine as you are today, always. Your smile, your enthusiasm and warmth uplift the lives of everyone around you.

THURSDAY	FRIDAY	SATURDAY	
			Nothing is so strong as gentleness; nothing so gentle as real strength. ST. FRANCIS DE SALES
Self-respect—that cornerstone of all virtue. JOHN HERSCHEL		*What is beautiful is moral, that is all there is to it.* FLAUBERT	**THE BEST THINGS THAT HAPPENED THIS WEEK:** ....
	The good lives on and does us all some good. RUTH GORDON		
			GOALS FOR NEXT WEEK: ❧............................ .... ❧............................ ....
When we become our own friend, we esteem ourselves. Self-respect is the armor of the soul.	*Good men and women continue to guide our course hundreds of years later. What good do you want to pass on to future generations?*	*True beauty is moral. Strive to make your world more beautiful.*	*A gentle person is not out to prove anything. That's true courage.*

Month _____		THE WEEK OF _____ TO _____	
	*S*UNDAY	*M*ONDAY	*T*UESDAY	*W*EDNESDAY

	SUNDAY	**MONDAY**	**TUESDAY**	**WEDNESDAY**
MORNING	*W*e don't know who we are until we see what we can do. MARTHA GRIMES			
NOON			*I* am at war 'twixt will and will not. SHAKESPEARE	
AFTERNOON				*H*onesty is the first chapter of the book of wisdom. THOMAS JEFFERSON
EVENING		*T*he great end of life is not knowledge but action. THOMAS HUXLEY		
GRACE NOTES	*S*elf-discovery comes through our actions. What is keeping you from doing all the exciting things you dream of? See what *you* can do. Know.	*K*nowledge alone is passive. Until you use your unique talents and bring something forth, you're wasting your life.	*I*ndecision cripples. Are you constantly changing your mind? Do you buy things and then return them? Choose. Don't wobble.	*I*'m nervous around people I can't trust. I sense something is off even when I'm being treacherously charmed. Honesty is essential.

Thursday	*Friday*	*Saturday*	
		… Grace upon grace … JOHN BOWEN COBURN	*I* slept and dreamt that life was joy. I woke and saw that life was duty. I acted, and behold! Duty was joy. RABINDRANATH TAGORE
	H old thou the good: define it well.　TENNYSON		**THE BEST THINGS THAT HAPPENED THIS WEEK:** ....
E verything we do has a result. GOETHE			**GOALS** **FOR NEXT WEEK:** ❧................................. .... ❧................................. ....
T here are consequences for every action. Think ahead. That's the definition of responsibility.	*F* ocus on goodness. What is good? How does it affect you? How does the lack of good make you feel? You always know good. True?	*G* race is a gift from God, freely given us. Be open and ready to receive grace. Count hundreds of grace notes every day.	*A* ll duty is an opportunity to serve, to give thanks, to give back and to appreciate. Use yourself well in duty. Joy always follows.

BIRTHDAYS AND CELEBRATIONS

January

DATE   EVENT

_____

_____

_____

_____

_____

_____

_____

_____

_____

_____

_____

_____

_____

February

DATE   EVENT

_____

_____

_____

_____

_____

_____

_____

_____

_____

_____

_____

_____

_____

March

DATE   EVENT

_____

_____

_____

_____

_____

_____

_____

_____

_____

_____

_____

_____

_____

July

DATE   EVENT

_____

_____

_____

_____

_____

_____

_____

_____

_____

_____

_____

_____

_____

August

DATE   EVENT

_____

_____

_____

_____

_____

_____

_____

_____

_____

_____

_____

_____

_____

September

DATE   EVENT

_____

_____

_____

_____

_____

_____

_____

_____

_____

_____

_____

_____

_____

April

DATE   EVENT

_____

_____

_____

_____

_____

_____

_____

_____

_____

_____

_____

May

DATE   EVENT

_____

_____

_____

_____

_____

_____

_____

_____

_____

_____

_____

June

DATE   EVENT

_____

_____

_____

_____

_____

_____

_____

_____

_____

_____

_____

October

DATE   EVENT

_____

_____

_____

_____

_____

_____

_____

_____

_____

_____

_____

November

DATE   EVENT

_____

_____

_____

_____

_____

_____

_____

_____

_____

_____

_____

December

DATE   EVENT

_____

_____

_____

_____

_____

_____

_____

_____

_____

_____

_____

CHILDREN'S, LOVERS', AND FRIENDS' FAVORITES

CHILD
FAVORITE THINGS

LOVER
FAVORITE THINGS

FRIEND
FAVORITE THINGS

CHILD
FAVORITE THINGS

LOVER
FAVORITE THINGS

LOVER
FAVORITE THINGS

FRIEND
FAVORITE THINGS

CHILD
FAVORITE THINGS

LOVER
FAVORITE THINGS

FRIEND
FAVORITE THINGS

CHILD

FAVORITE THINGS

_____

LOVER

FAVORITE THINGS

_____

FRIEND

FAVORITE THINGS

_____

FRIEND

FAVORITE THINGS

_____

CHILD

FAVORITE THINGS

_____

LOVER

FAVORITE THINGS

_____

FRIEND

FAVORITE THINGS

_____

CHILD

FAVORITE THINGS

_____

CHILD

FAVORITE THINGS

_____

LOVER

FAVORITE THINGS

_____

GIVING GIFTS

GIFT	FOR	WHERE PURCHASED	WHEN GIVEN

GIFTS READY TO GIVE!

GIFT   WHERE STORED

QUOTES, AFFIRMATIONS AND INSPIRATIONS

$\mathcal{L}$AUGHTER (Stories that made you laugh)

JOYS, SORROWS AND THINGS LEARNED

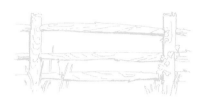

❦ _____

_____

_____

_____

_____

❦ _____

_____

_____

_____

_____

❦ _____

_____

_____

_____

_____

❦ _____

_____

_____

_____

_____

❦ _____

_____

_____

_____

_____

❦ _____

_____

_____

_____

_____

❦ _____

_____

_____

_____

_____

❦ _____

_____

_____

_____

_____

❧ _____
_____
_____
_____
_____

❧ _____
_____
_____
_____
_____
_____

❧ _____
_____
_____
_____
_____

❧ _____
_____
_____
_____

❧ _____
_____
_____
_____

❧ _____
_____
_____
_____
_____

❧ _____
_____
_____
_____
_____

❧ _____
_____
_____
_____

CARING, FOR YOURSELF ...

DOCTOR: _____

PHONE: _____

NOTES: _____

_____

DOCTOR: _____

PHONE: _____

NOTES: _____

_____

EYE DOCTOR: _____

PHONE: _____

NOTES: _____

_____

SPECIALIST: _____

PHONE: _____

NOTES: _____

_____

COUNSELOR: _____

PHONE: _____

NOTES: _____

_____

VETERINARIAN: _____

PHONE: _____

NOTES: _____

_____

DOCTOR: _____

PHONE: _____

NOTES: _____

_____

DENTIST: _____

PHONE: _____

NOTES: _____

_____

LAWYER: _____

PHONE: _____

NOTES: _____

_____

GYM/TRAINER: _____

PHONE: _____

NOTES: _____

_____

HAIRDRESSER: _____

PHONE: _____

NOTES: _____

_____

OTHER: _____

PHONE: _____

NOTES: _____

_____

AND *Your* Home

AUTO REPAIR: _____

PHONE: _____

NOTES: _____

_____

PLUMBER: _____

PHONE: _____

NOTES: _____

_____

ELECTRICIAN: _____

PHONE: _____

NOTES: _____

_____

HANDYMAN: _____

PHONE: _____

NOTES: _____

_____

PAINTER: _____

PHONE: _____

NOTES: _____

_____

YARD WORK: _____

PHONE: _____

NOTES: _____

_____

HOME INSURANCE: _____

PHONE: _____

NOTES: _____

_____

HARDWARE STORE: _____

PHONE: _____

NOTES: _____

_____

BANK: _____

PHONE: _____

NOTES: _____

_____

PHARMACY: _____

PHONE: _____

NOTES: _____

_____

SECURITY CO.: _____

PHONE: _____

NOTES: _____

_____

OTHER: _____

PHONE: _____

NOTES: _____

_____

$\mathcal{A}$SPIRATIONS

$\mathcal{B}$OOKS I HAVE READ

$\mathcal{B}$OOKS I WANT TO READ

NOTES

NOTES

NOTES